D0840584

GOOD NEWS STUDIES

Consulting Editor: Robert J. Karris, O.F.M.

Other Titles in Preparation

Being Poor

A Biblical Study

by

Leslie J. Hoppe, O.F.M.

Foreword
by
Archbishop Rembert G. Weakland, O.S.B.

Michael Glazier
Wilmington, Delaware

About the Author

Leslie Hoppe, OFM, is on the faculty of the Catholic Theological Union in Chicago. He is a graduate of the joint program in religion of Northwestern University and Garrett-Evangelical Theological Seminary. He received a Ph.D. from Northwestern University after completing a dissertation on the origins of the Book of Deuteronomy. Among his other publications is *Joshua, Judges, with Excursus on Charismatic Leadership in Israel.*

First published in 1987 by Michael Glazier, Inc., 1935 West Fourth Street, Wilmington, Delaware 19805.
©1987 by Michael Glazier, Inc.
Library of Congress Catalog Card Number: 87-45344.
International Standard Book Numbers:
  Good News Studies: 0-89453-290-1
  Being Poor: 0-89453-620-6
Typography by S. Almeida.
Printed in the United States of America.

TABLE OF CONTENTS

Foreword

No one could claim to belong to the Judeo-Christian ethical tradition without analyzing what role the poor and poverty itself play in that tradition. Perhaps we Christians, in particular, have become dulled to this concept because we have heard the texts concerning the poor so often that they no longer impress us. Perhaps, too, we simply have not found the strong passages of warning to the rich very helpful for us in the middle class and, thus, we have closed our eyes to them and the deeper meaning behind them. More than anything else, however, we have tried to spiritualize that concept in the light of Matthew's reading—"Blessed are the poor in spirit"—and have preferred to talk about spiritual poverty, considering material poverty of no importance except for religious.

Slowly we are becoming more aware of two sets of knowledge necessary for us if we wish to be disciples of Christ and understand the message of Scripture.

The first is an accurate knowledge of what terms meant in their original context. This is especially true for a concept such as "the poor." We must know how the term was used at different periods of the history of the people of God and what that people understood by the word. We must also understand the role such poor played in God's plan and their special role in the Kingdom. Leslie Hoppe's book is the kind of guide needed through the various uses of the term and what is meant in each context. It will be invaluable to all of us.

This knowledge will then have to be augmented by all the socio-historical studies being done about God's people and their neighbors in the various stages of their history. Such sociological studies are especially helpful for the use of the term in the New Testament.

With all this material at hand we can begin to grasp a little more fully the role of the poor in God's Kingdom and what that has to say to our present world and especially to the Church today.

It is important for us as community, first of all, to acquire such an awareness. It will affect our smaller parish community and its outreach. Since community now includes our solidarity with all on this globe, it can point out our obligations for mutual sharing on a much broader scale. But such studies will also have practical consequences for our personal spiritual life as well, because they help us reflect on how we should relate to material things and how we should distinguish between our real needs and all those other distracting wants that our culture thrusts at us. With such studies we may slowly be able to project a spirituality for our times that will measure success in terms other than the accumulation of wealth.

For all these reasons I welcome Leslie Hoppe's study as a serious contribution to a better understanding of the poor and their relationship to God's Kingdom. It will, thus, contribute also to a better understanding of what discipleship in the twentieth century is all about.

✠Rembert G. Weakland, O.S.B.
Archbishop of Milwaukee

Introduction

This book deals with a motif that is found throughout the Bible: the poor. The purpose of this study is to determine how the Bible can help individual believers and communities of faith shape their response to poverty today. One assumption behind this study is that the Bible can indeed tell us something important not only about spiritual concerns but material concerns as well, but anyone who begins to study what the Bible says about the poor will notice that there is a wide variety of affirmations made about poverty in the Bible. Sometimes poverty is a curse; other times it is a blessing. Sometimes the text is concerned exclusively about material poverty; other times poverty becomes a metaphor for another reality. The approach taken here is to describe the variety of ways the books which make up the Bible deal with the poor.

Obviously the biblical texts which speak about the poor cannot be detached from their historical, political and economic background without the very real danger of misunderstanding. For example, it makes quite a bit of difference whether the poor are spoken of by the wealthy or by the poor themselves. It matters very much whether "Blessed are you poor" was said by someone who was poor himself. In other words, it is important to know what was being said to whom and by whom. There should be no illusions about the objectivity of this approach. No method is really objective.

The interpreter's own perspectives can color texts which then can be used to undergird one's own previously held views. That is why readers ought to become actively involved in direct conversation with the texts under study.

One aim of this study has been to look at every text in the Bible where a word having "the poor" in its semantic field is found. Sometimes these texts were quoted in full but most often they are simply cited with the appropriate reference. Readers ought to look up these references and study these texts using this book as a way to enter into conversation with the Bible on their own. The readers' own experience may lead them to quite a different understanding of a particular text than the one presented by the author. One "objective" standard for authentic interpretation is to ask questions like the following: Has my understanding of this text given new direction to my conversion? Has it contributed to the vitality of the community of faith? Has it reshaped not only my attitudes but also my actions? Has it led to a deepening of my life of prayer?

Most of the book is devoted to texts from the Hebrew Scriptures. That should not be surprising since the bulk of the Christian Bible is taken up by these scriptures. In addition to canonical texts, the book contains references to intertestamental[1] and rabbinic texts. The intertestamental literature has been included to give a fuller picture of the religious and social situation which obtained at the time of Jesus' ministry and the emergence of the Church. The rabbinic material gives an idea of how a community of faith which considered itself the heir to traditions found in the Hebrew Bible appropriated and reinterpreted these traditions.

It is also important to know how responsible interpreters of the biblical tradition have understood specific texts. That is

---

[1]Intertestamental literature refers to Jewish religious texts composed during the three centuries between 200 B.C. and A.D. 100. Most of these texts have not been accepted as canonical by either the Jewish or Christian communities. They are sometimes called Old Testament Apocrypha and Pseudepigrapha. A good, popular introduction to this literature is Martin McNamara, M.S.C., *Intertestamental Literature* (Wilmington: Michael Glazier, 1983).

why bibliographical footnotes and a select bibliography at the end of each chapter have been included in this volume. This can help readers who may be unfamiliar with the secondary literature to become acquainted with the authors and works cited in this book. Hopefully this may facilitate the readers' study of this important biblical motif.

Finally a basic assumption that has colored this entire work is that "the poor" belong on the agenda of every community of faith. It is clear enough that ancient Israel, early Judaism, Jesus and the first Christians did not forget the poor. If believers today wish to be faithful to their biblical heritage, neither can they.

1

The Poor in the Tetrateuch

Introduction

The first four books of the Bible (the Tetrateuch) are made up of two elements: legislation and narration. The former presents the ideals of the community; the latter provides indications how these ideals shaped the perspectives of the people of Israel as these are revealed in their stories. For the most part, the legislation that deals with the poor reflects the agrarian economy of ancient Israel. People who did not own land and enjoy its productivity were in a very precarious economic situation. These were the poor. The legislation in the Torah deals with these people in two ways. First, it forbids the people of means from taking advantage of the situation in which the poor find themselves. Secondly, it describes ways whereby the wealthy could share their bounty with the poor. Undergirding all this legislation is the belief that God takes the side of the poor, that God is the protector of the poor, that God hears the cries of the poor. The narratives of the Tetrateuch illustrate these values. They show how ancient Israel's storytellers believed in a God who took the side of the poor.

The Legislation

In the traditions which were given their present shape by the Priestly Writer,[1] the poor are recognized as those who are without land and consequently without the means to feed themselves. For example, during the Sabbath year (Exod 23:11), the poor have no alternative but to try and survive on what grows wild on the ground which is left fallow while those who own land can live off what has been stored from the harvests of previous years. The priestly legislators are keenly aware of this disparity between the rich and the poor within the Israelite community for they require the people of means to help the landless without realizing any profit:

> "...if your brother becomes poor, and cannot maintain himself with you, you shall maintain him.... Take no interest from him or increase, but fear your God.... You shall not lend him your money at interest, nor give him your food for profit." (Lev 25:36-37)

When economic difficulties cause the poor to sell their labor, they are to be treated as hired servants and not slaves and their debts are to be forgiven and they are to be set free during the Year of Jubilee (Lev 25:39-43). At the time of harvest, the landowners are instructed to leave some of the fruits of their land to be picked by the poor (Lev 19:9-10; 23:22).

The priestly legislator is also aware that the poor cannot be expected to make the same type of offerings as the people of means. In the laws concerning sin offerings and the cleansing of lepers, special arrangements are made for those who cannot afford the usual sacrifices (Lev 5:7-13; 14:21-32).

---

[1]The term "the Priestly Writer" refers to the person who is responsible for the latest stratum of material used in the formation of the first four books of the Bible. This author is so named because the texts he is responsible for reflect a theological point of view which is characteristic of the Israelite priesthood.

The Covenant Code (Exod 20:22-23:33) is an example of ancient Israelite legal tradition which probably predates the rise of the monarchy. This code is particularly harsh on those who oppress the economically dependent. It comes to the defense of those who had to sell themselves into slavery for economic reasons (Exod 21:1-11, 21, 26-27). Israel's experience of the liberation brought by the Exodus ought to be a motive for justice (Exod 20:21). It assures Israel that God will move against those who harm widows and orphans with the result that the oppressor's own family will be reduced to poverty (Exod 22:21-24). The Code forbids the taking of interest on loans and limits the use a lender could have of a garment taken in pledge (Exod 22:26-27a). It asserts that Yahweh, the Compassionate, will hear the cries of the oppressed (Exod 22:27b). While this may be a rather negative form of motivation, it is intended to insure that the people of means will not ignore the poor. If they are ignored, God will hear their cries which will mean destruction for the wealthy. Finally, the code describes the Sabbath year when the fields were to lie fallow as an opportunity for the poor to eat:

> For six years you shall sow your land and gather in its yield: but the seventh year you shall let it rest and lie fallow, that the poor of your people may eat...." (Exod 23:10-11)

Of course, any enlightened legislation can be negated by a corrupt judiciary. That is why the legislation in the Book of the Covenant explicitly forbids the use of the courts to prevent justice for the poor: "You shall not pervert the justice due to your poor in his suit" (Exod 23:6). In fact, the entire series of laws in Exodus 23:1-9 may have originated to prevent the powerful and influential from keeping the poor from justice.[2]

---

[2]Exodus 23:3 reads "nor shall you be partial to a poor man in his suit." The word for poor here is *dl*. This could be emended to read *gdl*, "great one, influential one." A similar expression occurs in Leviticus 19:15 "...do not defer to the great..." The thrust of Exodus 23 is protecting the poor from the influential. There was little need for the latter to be protected from the former.

Before ending consideration of the legislation in the Tetrateuch it is important to consider the last of the Ten Commandments which prohibits covetousness:

> "You shall not covet your neighbor's house; you shall not covet your neighbor's wife, or his manservant, or his maidservant, or his ox, or his ass, or anything that is your neighbor's." (Exod 20:17)

This prohibition needs to be seen against the background of the ancient Israelite agricultural economy. If the economic status of farmers is precarious now, it was even more so in antiquity. A year with insufficient rains meant hardship; two years of drought meant disaster. The quality of the soil where the Israelites first settled was not the best. The Canaanites and later the Philistines controlled the fertile valleys and coastal plain. Then there was the ever present danger of raids (see Judg 6:1-6). After months of hard work, the harvest could be lost to bandit bands who preyed upon farmers. One way to get a hedge on the situation was to increase one's holdings. The more land one possessed, the greater likelihood of surviving the vagaries of the agricultural enterprise. But increasing one's holdings was always done at the expense of another. The tenth commandment warns against a kind of covetousness that could make poverty a permanent part of the Israelite social and economic scene. This becomes even more clear when a comparison is made with the version of that commandment given in Deuteronomy 5:21. In the latter text, the "field" is mentioned explicitly. The intended effect of the Tenth Commandment was to reverse the human tendency to self-interest and the desire to increase one's possessions and the security they provide at the expense of others.

The institution of the Sabbath Year, when the poor were able to glean from the fields and orchards that were not tended by their owners (Lev 25:1-7), was meant to ameliorate the conditions of those who failed as farmers. The Jubilee Year, when the ownership of forfeited land returned to the original families (Lev 25:8-55), was intended to reverse the slide into poverty. The legislation of the Tetrateuch then did not only require just treatment for the poor but it also provided for the means to keep poverty in check and even to eliminate it. Thus the Bible not only intends to prevent the unjust treatment of individual persons but also it legislates what can be called "structural" solutions to the problem of poverty. The legal traditions of ancient Israel looked upon poverty as an evil to be eliminated. These traditions did not hesitate to use the radical means of release from debt and the redistribution of property.[3] The theological basis of this legislation was that the ownership of Israel's land was vested in God—not in the land's human owners. This is the justification for the prohibition of selling any land in perpetuity. No human being had absolute control over the land for it belonged to God:

> "The land shall not be sold in perpetuity, for the land is mine [God's]; for you are strangers and sojourners with me." (Lev 25:23)

Secondly, laws of this kind reflected a belief that all Israel was a single family and the land was common property.[4]

---

[3]The Bible does not give direct evidence for the observance of these laws. Jeremiah, however, criticizes his contemporaries for not observing this law and says that Judah's coming defeat will be the result of this failure (Jer 34:8-37). The Jewish historian and apologist Josephus (1st century A.D.) remarks that the Sabbath year was observed in his time. After the First Revolt against Rome (A.D. 70) economic conditions were such that such observance was no longer possible. Roland De Vaux, O.P. maintained that the Jubilee Year was a late and ultimately vain attempt to radicalize the Sabbath Year by extending it to cover property. See his *Ancient Israel* (N.Y.: McGraw-Hill, 1961) pp. 175-177. Whether or not these laws were observed, they represented the belief that possessions were not owned by anyone absolutely.

[4]Sometimes the motivation for these laws is seen as a romantic reversion to the nomadic life in the wilderness as opposed to the settled life in Canaan. The wilderness was not idealized by the Israelites for the most part, though both Hosea (2:14-15) and Jeremiah (31:1-3) seem to do so. Usually the desert was seen as a place of evildoers and demons (Isa 13:21; 34:11-15). It was to the wilderness that the farmer Cain was exiled after he killed his brother Abel (Gen 4).

The legislation in the Tetrateuch is concerned about the poor but it does not idealize poverty. In fact, poverty is a curse that comes to those who do not observe the commandments of God (Lev 26:14-26). This shows that the people of ancient Israel looked upon poverty as abnormal—something that should not be. It is a curse.[5] The solutions to the problem of poverty are twofold: 1) there are strict safeguards which protect the poor from exploitation and 2) there are procedures designed to redistribute the wealth of ancient Israel to put an end to poverty.

The Narrative Tradition

The Patriarchal traditions (Gen 12-50) present the ancestors of Israel as people of means. Abraham especially is portrayed as a very wealthy man who had great flocks and herds, a large family and a great number of servants (Gen 13:2; 26:13-14). He had the wherewithal to engage in a war with four kings (see Gen 14:1-24). The Abraham tradition remembers how such a wealthy person can forget his responsibilities to those economically dependent upon him. When Abraham did forget Hagar, God took her side. At an early point in his adult life, Jacob is presented as an economically dependent person who had to resort to thievery in order to gain the recompense that was due him. But Jacob too became rich. Joseph, who eventually came to possess almost unlimited power in Egypt, found himself an imprisoned slave in that country. It was because God heard his prayers that Joseph was freed. Finally the Exodus traditions portray all the descendants of Israel as enslaved in Egypt. Because God heard their prayers in their need, they were delivered and led to a land of their own. Moses, their leader, is portrayed as exemplifying the kind of

---

[5]Other texts from the Bible deal with the theological problem which arises when it is clear that the poor person is not always a sinner nor is the wealthy person always just: Mic. 6:12; Job 21:7-12; Ps 73:1-4; Prov 16:8, 19; Sir 13:17-20.

attitude that is characteristic of those who like the poor are completely dependent upon God.

The story of Hagar and Ishmael (Gen 16:1-16) provides an example of the way God hears the cry of the afflicted. The barren Sarai gives her Egyptian maid, Hagar, to Abram. When Hagar becomes pregnant by Abram, Sarai accuses Hagar of insolence toward her and has her expelled from Abram's camp. Hagar is assured that God heard her call and that she will have a son Ishmael from whom the Arabs trace their descent. The point of this story is that God hears the plea of the mother of the Arabs who cries out because of the oppression she experienced at the hand of the mother of the Israelites. Oppression, no matter who is the perpetrator and who is the victim, is not ignored by God.

In the Jacob traditions, there are some stories about his stay with Laban, his kinsman and later his father-in-law. Upon leaving Laban, Rachel, the daughter of Laban and wife of Jacob, takes the images of her family's household gods.[6] When confronted by Laban with this theft, Jacob justifies this action as according to the Divine Will. Jacob maintains that Laban would have given Jacob nothing for his years of labor. God saw Jacob's plight and allowed him to get away with the household gods (Gen 31:17-42). While this story originated to show the quick wit and skill of the ancestors of the Israelites as compared with others, it does show that people of means had to be compelled to give what was due to those who were economically dependent upon them. If Laban had his way, Jacob would not have been compensated for his years of work.

---

[6]The significance of this act is not completely clear. At one time, it was believed that possession of the household gods signified legal title to property (see E. A. Speiser, *Genesis*. Anchor Bible, 1. [Garden City: Doubleday, 1964], p. 250). This conclusion was based on supposed parallels with second millennium documents from Nuzi which is located in modern Iraq. Recent study of these documents, however, have cast some doubt on earlier conclusions. See T. L. Thompson, *The Historicity of the Patriarchal Narratives* (Leiden: Brill, 1974) and M. J. Selman, "Comparative Customs and the Patriarchal Age" in *Essays on the Patriarchal Narratives*, A. R. Millard and D. J. Wiseman, eds. (Winona Lake, IN: Eisenbrauns, 1980), pp. 115-116.

Another story of God's vindication of the oppressed is the Joseph story (Gen 37-50). Though Joseph was sent to a life of slavery in Egypt by his jealous brothers and into prison because he rejected the advances of his master's wife, God responds to Joseph's cries of affliction and by a marvelous series of events raises him to a position second only to the Pharaoh. Joseph acknowledges as much when he names his son Ephraim: ". . . God has made me fruitful in the land of my affliction" (Gen 36:52).[7]

Of course, the most important event in ancient Israel's life was the Exodus which was a response God made to the oppression which the descendants of Abraham, Isaac and Jacob experienced at the hands of the Egyptians (Exod 3:7, 16-17; 4:31). If there was one lesson that Israel should have learned about Yahweh, it was that this God takes the side of the poor against those who cause their oppression.

In Numbers 12:3, Moses himself is described as having the basic attitude of the poor.[8] In this context, Moses is criticized by Miriam and Aaron because of his non-Israelite wife. Moses does not defend himself; rather, God defends Moses and strikes Miriam with leprosy. Moses' defender is God and God will always take the side of those who are dependent upon divine protection like the poor. Acceptance of this dependent status leads to a faithful submission to God which, in turn, gives Moses a special title to divine favor.[9]

Conclusion

The legislation of the Tetrateuch does not deal with the poor at any great length. The few texts that explicitly mention

[7]The name Ephraim is derived from a Hebrew word meaning "fruitful." God changed Joseph's situation from oppression to wealth.

[8]The English translations read ". . . Moses was very *meek*. . . " (Num 12:3). The word translated as meek is *'anaw*. It comes from the root *'nh*, which means "to be afflicted, oppressed." A related adjective *'ani* means "poor."

[9]This idea is important in a number of psalms. This does not mean that poverty as such is idealized as a state which gives one a special relationship with God. As this text shows, it is the attitude of dependence upon God which is decisive.

the poor show a compassion and a concern for the poor which is one hallmark of the biblical tradition. But this legislation is not satisfied with compassion; it requires a redistribution of property in order to eliminate poverty at its roots. Both these legal texts and the narrative texts are one in their conviction that the poor enjoy the special protection of God. It is incumbent upon all people of means, therefore, to imitate this divine concern. It should be noted that the legislation of the Bible regarding the poor is not unique. The culture of the ancient Near East is marked by its concern for the poor.[10] What is unique about ancient Israel's approach to poverty is the conviction that the land and its wealth belong to God— not to the human beings who happen to have temporary possession of it. This conviction leads to laws such as that of the Sabbath and Jubilee Years which have as their real aim the elimination of poverty.

Select Bibliography

Bailey, Lloyd R., *The Pentateuch.* Interpreting Biblical Texts. Nashville: Abingdon, 1981.

Burns, Rita J., *Exodus, Leviticus, Numbers.* The Old Testament Message, 3. Wilmington: Michael Glazier, 1983.

Childs, Brevard S., *The Book of Exodus.* The Old Testament Library. Philadelphia: Westminster, 1974.

De Vaux, Roland, *Ancient Israel.* 2 v. N.Y.: McGraw-Hill, 1961.

Millard, A. R. and Wiseman, D. J., eds., *Essays on the Patriarchal Narratives.* Winona Lake, IN: Eisenbrauns, 1980.

Vawter, Bruce, *On Genesis.* Garden City: Doubleday, 1977.

[10]A. Barucq, *Le Livre des Proverbes*, (Paris: Gabalda, 1964), pp. 33-34.

2

The Poor in the Book of Deuteronomy

Introduction

The Book of Deuteronomy presents itelf as the "constitution" governing ancient Israel's life in the land which was its inheritance from God (31:12-13). As such Deuteronomy deals with a whole range of religious, social, political and economic issues and institutions. One of the book's goals is to convince its readers that Israel's future depends solely on the quality of its loyalty to God (30:15-20). This loyalty is to be made explicit through the observance of traditional Israelite morality. The general tenor of this moral system and even many of its specific norms were already traditional practice extending in some instances to the pre-Israelite period. Indeed many of Deuteronomy's laws can be found in other Israelite legal codes. What makes Deuteronomy's presentation unique is its attempt to *persuade* and *motivate* its readers to obedience.

This approach is evident in Deuteronomy's treatment of the poor. Clearly most persons of means would have to be shown that it is to their advantage to be generous to the poor.

Though there have always been people who seem to be generous naturally, Deuteronomy is not content to leave the support of the poor to them. The book states that in theory there should be no poverty in the Israelite community: "But there will be no poor among you..." (15:4a). In a more realistic vein, the book attempts to move people of means to aid the poor whose numbers never seem to diminish: "For the poor will never cease out of the land; therefore, I command you, you shall open wide your hand to your brother, to the needy and to the poor, in the land" (15:11).

Deuteronomy deals with poverty primarily by exhorting the wealthy to ignore their own self-interest by depriving themselves of what is theirs in order to supply the needs of the poor. The result of such a course of action is beneficial not only to the poor but to their benefactors as well since benevolence to the poor is commanded by God. Obedience to God's commandments always brings blessings. Disobedience, in this case acting purely out of self-interest, creates disaster because acting purely out of self-interest leads to acts of injustice which prompt God to move against those responsible (e.g. 24:14-15).[1]

Laws Regarding the Poor

Explicit references to the poor in Deuteronomy are few: 15:4, 7, 9, 11; 24:12, 14, 15.[2] The first four of these appear in the legislation regarding the year of release (15:1-11); the last three in laws dealing with loans to the poor (24:10-13 and 14-15).

[1]Deuteronomy threatens poverty to those who are not obedient: 28:48, 57. Thus a disobedient Israel will be made to be poor.

[2]The word for the poor in these texts is *'ebyon*. The word refers to someone who wants something which he does not have, and consequently a person who is needy and poor. See G. H. Botterweck, "*'ebhyon*," in *Theological Dictionary of the Old Testament*. G. J. Botterweck and H. Ringgren, eds. (Grand Rapids: Eerdmanns, 1974), p. 28.

THE YEAR OF RELEASE (15:1-11)

A basic Israelite belief was that though God gave the land to Israel, it really belonged to the Lord who gave it as a gift to Israel in accordance with the promises made to Israel's ancestors (11:8-12). An important consequence of this belief was a recognition of Israel's dependence upon God's bounty. The wealthy and the poor alike were to acknowledge God as the source of their sustenance. One way that Israel chose to express this belief was through the customs surrounding the year of release.

The law dealing with the year of release probably had its origin with the practice of allowing the land to lie fallow at regular intervals (see Exod 23:10-11 and Lev 25:2-7). Obviously the observance of such a custom would have been staggered throughout Israel, but each time it was observed by an individual farmer the fallow year made life hard for those economically dependent upon agriculture. Certainly they would have found repaying any outstanding debts extremely difficult. One purpose of the forerunner of the Deuteronomic law was to prohibit the calling in of debts during a farmer's fallow year, though Deuteronomy required that the debt be forgiven rather than simply deferred. The "foreigner" spoken of in 15:3 is not the resident alien, who was somewhat integrated into the Israelite economic and agricultural system, but probably the traveling merchant or craftsman, who was not affected by the fallow year.[3] The law makes it clear that no one was to take advantage of another's financial difficulties. The poor were to experience the generosity of their fellow Israelites (15:9-11).

Because of the practical problems associated with the observance of the fallow year, this custom fell into disuse. Nowhere does Deuteronomy make any mention of the Fallow or Sabbath Year though the legislation in Exodus and Leviticus still refers to that ancient custom. Deuteronomy, in a real sense, updates an ancient law by breaking its ties with a no

---

[3]Deuteronomy uses three words in the semantic field "foreign, strange, alien." The one used here refers to non-Israelites who were simply traveling through the country. They were not the resident aliens who had many more rights.

longer observed agricultural custom while retaining its concern for those with financial problems. More than this, Deuteronomy tries to eliminate the possibility of a debtor class in the Israelite community by requiring the cancellation of all debts owed by one Israelite to another at the end of every seventh year. Deuteronomy then is not just calling for charity but it is trying to insure that Israelite society will not be divided *permanently* into two classes: the economically powerful and the economically dependent.

The kind of loans that this Deuteronomic law has in mind is one which involved the pledge of personal services as security against non-payment. Apparently creditors were within their legal rights to compel delinquent debtors to become bond servants in the case of default. Deuteronomy not only requires that the debt be cancelled but in effect it also frees those who had become bond servants in order to work off their debts. So that the source of loans to the poor would not dry up, the law enjoins people of means to lend to those in need even as the year of release approached (v. 8). Failure to be generous to the poor is described as an evil with the use of the formula: "...and it be sin in you" (v. 9b). Deuteronomy uses the same formula to condemn the withholding of the wages of the poor (see 24:15b). The assumption behind this negative motivation is that help for the poor should be forthcoming from the people of means. Any failure in this regard brings divine judgment upon the Israelite community since God is the defender of the poor.

After the law of release is given in vv. 1-3, there follows a description of the blessings that will come to Israel if this law is observed (vv. 4-6). Here is one place where Deuteronomy tries to move its readers to obedience. The result of compliance will be nothing less than the elimination of poverty in the land which was Israel's inheritance from God (v. 4). Also Israel's prosperity will be such that it can offer loans to other nations (v. 6). Israel, however, is told never to seek financial assistance from other nations since such a course of action would be a breach of faith in God who not only will provide for Israel's material needs but will even eliminate poverty if Israel were obedient. This approach is typical of Deuteronomy which does not simply state laws which are to be observed but also seeks to move its readers to obedience by providing motives for observance.

Another typically Deuteronomic characteristic is the assumption that *all Israelites* belong to *one family*. This passage refers to the poor as "brothers" of the wealthy no less than six times in the 11 verses that make up the law of release (vv. 2, 3, 7 [2x], 9, 11).⁴ That some members of the one family of Israel be without the material blessings promised to all is just not right according to Deuteronomy. Of course, the authors of this text were realistic enough to recognize that the kind of obedience needed to bring an end to poverty would not be forthcoming from Israel. That is why the book calls so strongly for generosity toward the poor (v. 11). Deuteronomy fails to find any positive value in poverty. It is never described as a state which places one in closer proximity to God; rather, the deprivation of material blessings enjoyed by the wealthy is an evil which must be eliminated by means of generous actions on the part of people who themselves enjoyed these blessings.⁵

This law makes it clear that Deuteronomy understands the poor person as one without the kind of material prosperity that allows for economic security. The poor are those who need the economic support of others. Occasionally the needs of the poor become so acute that they will be forced into bond slavery by their creditors. Such a situation was not to become permanent within the Israelite community, otherwise a socio-economic rift would develop within the Israelite community that could destroy it. Deuteronomy envisions a community whose members understand themselves as members of a

⁴The word "brother" is Deuteronomy's usual expression in referring to the members of the Israelite community regardless of their social status: 1:10; 3:18, 20; 10:9, 19; 15:3, 7, 9, 11; 17:15; 18:2.

⁵Apparently Deuteronomy reflects a socio-economic situation which the Deuteronomists see as able to be improved. The gap betweeen rich and poor had not become so wide as to become unbridgeable. If Hanson's thesis is correct (see his *The Dawn of Apocalyptic* [Philadelphia: Fortress, 1975]), eventually this gap became so wide as to lead some people to give up on the possibilities of justice in this world. Deuteronomy's perspectives clearly assume that justice for the poor is something that is not only possible in this world but also the will of God for the world.

single family and act accordingly. Such an attitude and behavior could effectively eliminate poverty in the Israelite community.

Finally, in characterizing the unwillingness to aid the poor as a sin (v. 9), Deuteronomy asserts that Israel's relationship with God was a product of the intersocietal relationships that existed among the Israelites themselves. Traditions with a more pronounced cultic orientation like those behind the Chronicler[6] seemed to assume that Israel's relationship with God was determined by ritual activity. While Deuteronomy does not ignore this approach to the Divine, it chooses to emphasize a view of religion that sees the relationship between God and Israel as determined by the quality of human relationships among the Israelites themselves. This approach to religion seems paradoxical but it is no more so than the promise that the enjoyment of the land and its material blessings rests upon the readiness of the wealthy to relinquish them (vv. 4-6, 10). Perhaps Deuteronomy here reflects a perspective on Israel's loss of the land as a result of the Babylonian Exile that understood that loss as the result of social conflict that pitted rich against poor.[7]

LOANS TO THE POOR (23:19-20; 24:6, 10-13)

Another Deuteronomic passage which specifically mentions the poor is the law regarding pledges (24:10-13). Again this text is reminiscent of a law in Exodus that deals specifically with garments taken as collateral for a loan which is to be interest-free (Exod 22:26-27). It forbids keeping such a garment overnight because of the hardship this would cause. Deuteronomy adds another specification: creditors may not enter their debtors' homes in order to secure their collateral. Deuteronomy's concern is to maintain the dignity of the poor

---

[6]"The Chronicler" is the name given to the individual or school responsible for 1 and 2 Chronicles, Ezra and Nehemiah. Similar theological interests and literary features characterize these books.

[7]Admittedly this is not made explicit in Deuteronomy though the formula "...and it be sin in you" (15:9b; 24:15b) intimates that the consequences of failure to help the poor are more than social and economic.

in what was already a humiliating situation. To allow creditors inside the homes of their debtors in order to rummage about for a suitable item to take as collateral was demeaning to the families that found themselves in severe economic need. Keeping creditors outside the home of their debtors preserves at least a modicum of dignity and self-respect for the poor. This is another example of Deuteronomy's humanizing efforts.

After the proviso about collateral in general, Deuteronomy then deals with the case of a poor person's garment taken in pledge for a loan (vv. 12-13). Deuteronomy follows the lead of Exodus by requiring that creditors must return garments taken in pledge before nightfall. Deuteronomy is even more pointed in its legislation since it specifically forbids creditors from sleeping in the pledged garment. Persons would have to be quite poor if they had to give over that portion of their clothing which was needed to ward off the night chill. In such cases, people needing loans probably had nothing else of value to offer as security for the loan. Both Exodus and Deuteronomy require that debtors be treated with charity. While Exodus implies divine retribution if its command is ignored by creditors (Exod 22:27b), Deuteronomy takes a more positive approach. For the Deuteronomists[8] the consequence of treating the poor with understanding is a blessing from the poor which will, in turn, bring with it divine approval (Deut 24:13). Here again, Deuteronomy shows that it conceives of the relationship between God and Israel as a by-product of good intersocietal relationships among the members of the Israelite community. Sensitivity and understanding toward the poor bring about a kind of harmony within society that results in nothing less than God's righteousness.

One other text dealing with collateral is related to issues under study here even though it does not mention the poor

---

[8]This term refers to those who are responsible for the Book of Deuteronomy. There is some debate regarding the origins of this book though it is clear that those responsible for it consider their work to be the definitive and authoritative summary of the Mosaic tradition.

explicitly. In 24:6 creditors are forbidden to ask that a family's millstone be surrendered in order to secure a loan. Without a millstone, grain cannot be ground to prepare bread, the staple in the ancient Israelite diet. Demanding such collateral would involve hardship for any family—especially a poor one.

Finally Deuteronomy specifies that loans be interest-free (23:19-20). The loans envisoned here have no resemblance to the loaning practices that are central to a modern capitalist economy. In ancient Israel loans were not taken out in order to raise capital for economic expansion. In the situation addressed by Deuteronomy, loans are used only as a means to escape economic disaster. To take advantage of partners in the covenantal community when they are in financial distress is incompatible with Deuteronomy's view of community. Loans made to those outside the community are another matter.[9] God will give adequate provision to all Israel if the community is faithful to the Law. There should be no need to supplement God's gracious bounty with interest earned on loans to brothers and sisters in financial need. Again though the poor are not mentioned by name, Deuteronomy surely has them in mind with this legislation.

THE WAGES OF THE POOR (24:14-15)

The Holiness Code[10] specifically forbids withholding the wages of the day laborer (Lev 19:13). In fact, the law from Leviticus equates this practice with robbery and oppression. Deuteronomy, as is its usual practice, expands on this traditional piece of legislation. It describes the laborers in question as "poor and needy" (v. 14). Clearly such persons

[9]Deuteronomy tends to have a narrow perspective when it comes to dealing with non-Israelites. See 23:4-9. Though the book consistently urges consideration for the resident alien and includes them with the widows and orphans as fit objects for the charity of the Israelites, its focus is primarily on the relationship of the Israelite poor with the people of means who belonged to the same community.

[10]"The Holiness Code" is the name which has become applied to Leviticus 17-26. This law code is distinguished by its hortatory style, its concern for moral conduct and cultic purity and, above all, by its use of the divine first person (see Leviticus 19:2; 20:26).

would find it difficult to forego their wages until their employers deem it convenient to make payment. The poor need what little wages they earn to avoid going hungry. Deuteronomy extends its protection in this instance to the resident alien as well. Perhaps it is because the Deuteronomist is familiar with the tradition behind Exodus 22:21-24 which forbids the exploitation of aliens.

Again the Deuteronomist uses the formula "...and it will be sin in you" (v. 14) to underscore the seriousness of this law. Also the warning of v. 15 ("...lest he cry against you to the Lord...") intimates that God takes the side of the poor against those who take advantage of them. This is a point made explicitly in Exodus 22:3. Deuteronomy simply allows its readers to draw their own conclusions about the consequences of disobedience when it states that withholding of wages is a sin. Now sin, if it is serious enough, can be punished by death in the view of the Deuteronomist: 21:22; 22:26; 24:16. Usually though Deuteronomy is less interested in the fate of individuals than with that of the community as a whole. The basic thrust of this law is toward preventing the kind of abuse that makes the cycle of poverty something that cannot be broken. Withholding the wages of the poor makes their poverty all the more burdensome—and unnecessarily so. It will also cause them to go into debt in order to survive when they should be able to enjoy the fruits of their labor. Withholding the wages of the poor makes it impossible to break the cycle of poverty and to heal the economic divisions of Israelite society.

Breaking the Cycle of Poverty

In the texts which mention the poor explicitly, Deuteronomy seeks to eliminate the exploitation of those who are rendered especially vulnerable to abuse because of their precarious economic situation. The book, however, takes additional steps to prevent conditions from developing which could serve only to breed poverty. Deuteronomy is convinced that poverty is not something inevitable but the result of human decisions to live contrary to the expressed will of God. If Israel were obedient, poverty simply would not exist (15:4). Despite belief in this ideal, Deuteronomy is realistic enough to foresee the need for being as specific as possible in opposing the kind of social, economic and political patterns of behavior that make poverty an inescapable component of the social system (15:11).

DEPENDENT PERSONS

The first group of laws that will be considered are those which deal with economically marginalized groups. For a variety of reasons, some people find themselves out of the economic mainstream. The Deuteronomists are aware of this and focus their attention on these people. They call for specific action to prevent the precarious position of the marginalized from degenerating. The purpose of Deuteronomy's legislation is to place these dependent people on a more secure economic basis. To accomplish this the Deuteronomists do not hesitate to call upon the generosity of the wealthy.

Widows, Orphans and Aliens (10:18; 14:29; 16:11, 14; 24:17, 19-21)

The peoples of the ancient Near East believed that widows, orphans and other groups without economic power were under special divine protection.[11] Because these people were generally unable to own land which was the basis of economic security in the agricultural economy of the ancient Near East, they were in an especially vulnerable position. As a representative of the gods, the king was required to protect the people who were without a secure economic basis to protect themselves. In accord with these perspectives, Deuteronomy too sees these people as under the special protection of Israel's

---

[11]F. Charles Fensham, "Widow, Orphan and the Poor in Ancient Near Eastern Legal and Wisdom Literature," *Journal of Near Eastern Studies* 21 (1962) 129-139.

God: "God executes justice for the fatherless and the widow, and loves sojourners, giving them food and clothing" (10:18). This statement about the character of God has implications for Israel's behavior. God's particular concern for those in the community whose social and economic state was insecure ought to move all Israel to insure that these people receive just and proper treatment. Deuteronomy then widens the circle of responsibility for the welfare of these people from God and the king to all people of means. Deuteronomy wishes to protect these economically dependent groups from the kind of exploitation that is so easily accomplished and so difficult to undo because the widow, orphan and alien were outside the economic and sometimes the judicial mainstream. Deuteronomy commends these people to the care of their more well-to-do neighbors. Their generosity can prevent the cycle of poverty from becoming a continuously downward spiral.

The Levites (12:12, 17-18; 14:27, 29; 16:11; 18:1-8)

Deuteronomy shows a special concern for the Levites, i.e. those who were the priests of local sanctuaries that the book's law of centralization (12:2-6) rendered illegitimate as sites of sacrificial worship. One consequence of the centralization of Israel's worship in the Temple of Jerusalem was that the Levites, who had no land from which to gain support, would now be deprived of their liturgical role along with its related benefices. In effect, Deuteronomy created another economically dependent group. That is why the book adds the Levites to the traditional three economically dependent groups (see 14:29; 16:11, 14). The Deuteronomists do not hesitate to commend the Levites to the charity of their fellow Israelites (12:2, 17-18; 14:27).

Special attention needs to be given to 18:1-8. This is the only place in Deuteronomy where the book concerns itself with cultic personnel apart from some occasion when a lay person would have some reason to deal with them. Verses 6-8 are clearly intended to provide the Levites with an opportunity to serve in the one remaining legitimate sanctuary and thereby derive some support from their liturgical role. This was not a very practical solution to the problems created by centralization. There were, after all, many local sanctuaries once served by Levites but according to Deuteronomy's legislation there was only one legitimate place for sacrificial worship. This lone sanctuary could never support all the Levites in the land. A similar solution to the Levites' problem failed in an earlier attempt at centralization tried by Josiah (see 2 Kgs 23:9). Eventually the problems of the Levites were solved to some extent when they became a type of second-rank clergy (see Ezek 44:9-14) but the Deuteronomists were not responsible for this arrangement. The best they were able to do was to commend the Levites to the charity of their fellow Israelites. Hopefully a positive response could prevent the Levites from swelling the ranks of the "poor and needy."

Slaves (15:12-18; 23:15-16)

Israelite bond slaves served no more than seven years. The law of release (15:1-11) freed the poor from the debts and obligations to their creditors. Similar provisions are found in the Covenant Code (Exod 22:1-12). The most significant difference in Deuteronomy's legislation is the requirement that generous provision be made for the freed bond slave:

> "And when you let him go free from you, you shall not let him go empty-handed; you shall furnish him liberally...as the Lord your God has blessed you, you shall give to him."
> (15:13-14)

Once slaves had claimed their freedom, their former masters were to help them make a smooth transition to freedom. Without such help, the former slaves will eventually find that their newly acquired freedom brought them to the same kind of destitution that led them to bond slavery in the first place. Deuteronomy wished to break the cycle of poverty that kept the poor in impossible economic situations.

Unique to Deuteronomy, the law regarding escaped slaves (23:15-16) is stated in an unusually succinct manner. One consequence of this terseness is a question regarding the scope of the law. Is the law intended to apply to slaves who flee to Israel from foreign countries (see 1 Kgs 2:39-40)? Does it forbid cooperation in extradition proceedings against escaped slaves? Perhaps this law is intended to apply to the situation when a slave flees from an Israelite master and seeks refuge among other Israelites. The law is not very specific regarding its scope. In some ancient Near Eastern treaties, provisions were made for the return of fugitive slaves,[12] but Deuteronomy opposes such action. The runaway slave is to go free. Perhaps the Deuteronomists considered slavery to be an embarrassment because it was out of line with the basic thrust of its own religious perspectives and Israel's sacred traditions about the God who *frees* slaves (5:15). Deuteronomy takes this opportunity to weaken slavery's hold. Not only will the slave be freed after seven years of service (15:12-16) but runaway slaves are not to be returned. These two provisions effectively undermined the foundations of bond slavery, an institution which hardly corresponds to the Deuteronomic image of Israel as a community of brothers and sisters. Likewise Deuteronomy's setting is precisely that point in Israel's life when it was making its transition from slavery into freedom. There ought to be little wonder then at the book's treatment of bond slavery. What is perplexing is the book's failure to condemn this practice outright as incompatible with Israel's divinely ordered pattern of life. Perhaps conditions were such that bond slavery was an almost inescapable part of Israel's social and economic system.

FEEDING THE POOR

The most pressing concern for the poor is survival itself. Having enough food to survive is first on their agenda. Deuteronomy is careful to insure that the poor have food available to them. In addition to the requirement that the dependent

---

[12]See *Ancient Near Eastern Texts Relating to the Old Testament*, [*ANET*] 3rd ed. James B. Pritchard, ed. (Princeton, N.J.: Princeton University Press, 1955), pp. 200-203.

classes share in the meals associated with the pilgrimage festivals (16:11, 14), Deuteronomy specifies two other ways through which the poor share in the agricultural bounty of the land. The first of these is the triennial tithe which, unlike the annual tithe, is not brought to the central sanctuary but is to be made available to the dependent groups in each locality (14:22-29). The second is the law which allows the dependent classes to have some share in the harvest of grain, olives and grapes (24:19-22).

The Triennial Tithe (14:28-29)

This tithe is Deuteronomy's attempt to provide relief for the poor on a regular basis. It is similar to the requirement of the fallow year in Exodus 23:10-11 which had the benefit of the poor as its purpose. The latter law, which requires the release of an entire year's harvest, may have been too impractical to have been observed for very long once the Israelite economy became more complex. Deuteronomy's specification of a tithe is a bit more realistic in its expectations regarding support for people without land of their own. What Deuteronomy was trying to accomplish by means of this law was the welfare of the poor. Originally the custom of tithing had mythological and ritual associations. The tithe was an offering of a tenth portion of the harvest to the divine owner of the land through a sacrificial rite that insured the continued fertility of the soil. In the ancient Near East generally the tithe became a means of supporting a sanctuary. Here there is none of that in evidence. From being an obligatory gift to the gods the tithe has become an obligatory gift to the poor.[13]

---

[13]In commenting on this text Gerhard von Rad states: "From the standpoint of old conceptions of a sacrifice this is an astonishing rationalization of cultic usage!" See his *Deuteronomy* (Philadelphia: Westminster, 1966) p. 103. Here Deuteronomy clearly "humanizes" an ancient cultic usage. Deuteronomy is able to do this because its law of centralization eliminates the need to support a large number of sanctuaries. The Deuteronomist is able to transform this traditional practice into a means to support the poor rather than to support sanctuaries.

The Harvest (24:19-22)

Apparently the custom of not harvesting a field completely was an ancient one. Perhaps it originated as a way to placate the spirits of the field in order to secure continued good harvests.[14] The Holiness Code is aware of this custom but, of course, it supplies a different motivation: the welfare of the poor (Lev 19:9-10; 23:22). Here Deuteronomy specifies the same. Rabbinic commentators have noted two unusual features in this legislation.[15] First, obedience to this law offers *little real help* to the poor and, secondly, the owners of the fields do not even intend to help the poor since the poor receive a share in the harvest only if the farmers *forget* to bring the entire harvest into their storehouses. These two features of the law led rabbinic interpreters to the conclusion that the precept is not specifically aimed at benefitting the poor but at forming the character of the person of means. The law reminded farmers that the land and its bounty are theirs only in trust from God. Successful farmers should not think that their harvests belong to them but rather they belong to the poor as well. This command is to promote a generous attitude on the part of the wealthy. What better example of generosity is there than that of people who give to the poor without knowing to whom they are giving and without the recipients knowing from whom it comes? The distinctive feature of this precept seems to lie in the unconscious character of its implementation. In sum, this precept calls for the abdication of absolute proprietorship on the part of the wealthy.

THE JUDICIAL AND POLITICAL SPHERES

Two other laws are intended by the Deuteronomists as safeguards to prevent conditions from developing which could serve to make poverty an inevitable component of the Israelite social order. The first of these is the requirement of righteous

---

[14]At least this is von Rad's suggestion, see his *Deuteronomy*, p. 152.

[15]See the discussion in N. Leibowitz, *Studies in Devarim* (Jerusalem: WZO, 1980) 243-249.

judgment (1:9-18; 16:18-20) and the second is the law of the king (17:14-20). Neither of these laws explicitly mentions the poor but nothing can facilitate the destruction of the social order as much as a corrupt judicial and political system, as is evident from the prophetic criticism of these institutions. The perversion of the monarchy and the judiciary helped create and maintain poverty. This Israel learned through harsh experience. Deuteronomy's hope for Israel gives rise to specific legislation on what must be done to keep these two institutions free from the kind of corruption that affects the poor most of all.

The Judiciary (1:9-18; 16:18-20)

The first passage (1:9-18) is a narrative account of the appointment of Israel's judiciary by Moses. The second (16:18-20) is a legal text requiring Israel to appoint its judiciary. The narrative makes it clear that justice is to be done for both the Israelite and the alien (1:16). The dependent status of aliens makes them even more liable to injustice than native Israelites. The same verse refers to the Israelites as "brothers," which is Deuteronomy's characteristic manner of referring to members of the Israelite community.[16] This kind of language ignores the kind of social stratification brought about by economic differences among people. Deuteronomy seems to favor a kind of equality that is incompatible with significant differences in economic prosperity. That is why careful administration of the judicial office is so crucial to Deuteronomy's conception of what Israel is to be.

The Deuteronomic law on the appointment of judges (16:18-20) is similar to that in the Covenant Code (Exod 23:6-8). The scope of the law in Exodus is wider than that in Deuteronomy because the former is not directed at judges alone but prohibits anyone from perverting the judicial system. Deuteronomy 16:19b is almost a verbatim repetition of Exodus 23:8 except for the substitution of "wise" in Deuteronomy for the "officials" of the Exodus text. The text

---

[16]See no. 4.

concludes with a typical Deuteronomic rhetorical pattern: following a prohibition with a positive command. In this case the prohibition against taking a bribe is followed by the command to do justice (v. 20).

The Law of the King (17:14-20)

The same kind of language (Israelites=brothers) and the same kind of concern for equality within the Israelite community mark Deuteronomy's law of the king. According to this text, God gives permission for Israel to have a king under certain conditions. The conditions of a negative nature are given in vv. 16-17. The one positive condition is that the king study and observe the Law (v. 19). The purpose of these conditions, both positive and negative, is to prevent the Israelite monarchy from becoming an institution that models and facilitates economic and social stratification. Leaving aside the question of the law's practicality,[17] one ought to be able to recognize Deuteronomy's social idealism here. More than any other institution in Israel's life, the monarchy brought within its wake social stratification and economic circumstances that made poverty almost inevitable. Samuel's speech warning against the evils of the monarchy (1 Sam 8:10-18) and the Naboth incident (1 Kgs 21:1-24) are two of the Deuteronomistic tradition's[18] more dramatic illustrations of just that. Here Deuteronomy's view of a more equitable social system is quite obvious. If only the king would study and observe the Law, poverty would not exist, since the observance of the Law is a guarantee against poverty (15:4). If Israelite society is inconceivable without the monarchy, the Deuteronomists will accept this institution as long as it is subject to the Law whose observance insures the prosperity and welfare of all.

---

[17]No ancient Near Eastern monarch would ever consent to rule in accordance with its provisions.

[18]The term "deuteronomistic" is used to describe the theological interests and literary style characteristic of the Book of Deuteronomy, which had a significant role to play in the editing of the Books of Joshua, Judges, Samuel and Kings. This tradition will be the subject of the next chapter.

Conclusion

Deuteronomy never intimates that there is any positive value in poverty.[19] On the contrary, Deuteronomy asserts that poverty is something that does not belong in the Israelite community (15:4). It is a curse on a disobedient Israel (28:29b). The continued presence of the community in its land is dependent upon the maintenance of just intersocietal relationships. In fact, Israelites ought to relate to one another as members of the same family. That some members of that family enjoy material benefits that others do not is a hollow kind of familial relationship. It is a situation that Deuteronomy tries to eliminate. The book calls upon the Israelites of means to relieve the burdens of the poor and to direct their community's life in such a way as to combat some of the causes of poverty.

The first step in accomplishing these goals entails a call to the wealthy to renounce their rights and claims upon the poor. No interest is to be taken on loans (23:19-20), the poor are to be released from their debts periodically (15:1-6), a released bond servant is to be treated with generosity (15:12-18) and forgotten sheaves from the harvest are to be left for the poor (24:17-22). Deuteronomy asks people of means to follow a course of action which is contrary to their self-interest but which assures them that the results of such behavior will be of ultimate benefit because they secure God's blessings and continued possession of the land. Deuteronomy recognizes that unmitigated self-interest breeds injustice and that the only way to secure God's blessings is to share them.

Deuteronomy's approach to the issue of poverty is not simply to legislate but to motivate. The book does so by implying that the quality of Israel's relationship with God is a by-product of just intersocietal relationships. Failure to achieve such relationships is a sin (15:9; 24:15). Another tack taken by Deuteronomy is to characterize intersocietal relationships as familial. After all, the covenant not only binds Israel to God

---

[19]von Rad, *Deuteronomy*, pp. 106-107.

but it binds individuals together in one family, the Israelite community. Poverty ought not to exist in a community made up of brothers and sisters (15:4). Indeed it would not if all Israel were obedient to the law. If poverty does exist then it is not because it is inevitable according to the laws of economics or because of some failure on the part of the poor. Poverty is the result of human decisions to ignore the Law. This human failure is what is inevitable, so poverty will exist within the Israelite community (15:11). In the light of this reality, the book takes some specific steps to help those who find themselves out of the economic mainstream.

Deuteronomy makes all sorts of calls for sensitive and caring behavior toward the economically dependent. Certainly the book could have gone beyond the few situations it specifies but enough is said to insure that Israel hears this message: the land and its wealth belong to no one absolutely. Along with the material blessings enjoyed by the wealthy comes the responsibility to care for those with special economic needs. Above all no one should go hungry (14:28-29; 24:19-22). The fruitfulness of the land is such that all can share in its bounty.

There are any number of ways to deal with the problem of poverty—from revolution to spiritualization. Deuteronomy's vision of Israel as a family makes revolution an unacceptable alternative. Similarly Deuteronomy refuses to eliminate the scandal of poverty by "elevating" it to a state of special closeness to God. Deuteronomy makes the alleviation of the suffering of the poor a matter of obedience to the divine will. If Israel would abide by the law, there would be no poverty. Because people have failed to be obedient, poverty is a reality that needs to be handled. Deuteronomy speaks to the prosperous, to judges, to owners of bond slaves, to creditors, to all who are in a position to either mitigate or worsen the situation of the poor. The Deuteronomists demand that the basic needs of the poor be tended to and that the institutions of society function in such a way as to lessen their burdens. The Deuteronomists know that the one way to facilitate this is to ask that people of means relinquish some of their "rights," act against their own economic self-interest and treat the poor as members of their own families which, in reality, they are.

Select Bibliography

Clifford, Richard, S. J., *Deuteronomy*. The Old Testament Message, 4. Wilmington: Glazier, 1982.

McConville, J. G., *Law and Theology in Deuteronomy*. Sheffield, England: The University of Sheffield, 1983.

Mayes, A. D. H., *Deuteronomy*. The New Century Bible Commentary. Grand Rapids: Eerdmans, 1981.

Rad, Gerhard von, *Deuteronomy*. The Old Testament Library. Philadelphia: Westminster, 1966.

3

The Poor in the Former Prophets

Introduction

The books known as the Former Prophets (Joshua, Judges, Samuel and Kings) in rabbinic tradition tell the story of how Israel came first to possess the land promised to its ancestors and then to lose that land. The theological perspectives which undergird the telling of this tragic story are taken from the Book of Deuteronomy; hence, these books have also come to be known as the Deuteronomistic History of Israel.[1] The Book of Deuteronomy is concerned with motivating Israel to the observance of traditional Yahwistic moral values. The Deuteronomistic History is an extended object-lesson in what happens when Israel lived in accordance with those values and what happened when Israel chose to live otherwise.

In this chapter, besides considering the texts that explicitly deal with the poor, we will consider how the Deuteronomists

---

[1]The first to propose the theory of a Deuteronomistic History was Martin Noth. See his *Deuteronomistic History*. Journal for the Study of the Old Testament Supplement Series, 15. (Sheffield: University of Sheffield, 1981). Though there have been many developments of this theory since Noth first proposed it in 1943, most interpreters of the Former Prophets use Noth's theory as a working hypothesis in their own studies of these texts.

tell their story of Israel by focusing on issues of poverty, oppression, injustice as they were manifested in ancient Israel's life in the land. In a sense, the Deuteronomistic History is the story of how Israel acquired and then lost the land. What happened to the poor is really at the center of that story.

The Pre-monarchic Situation: Joshua and Judges

The Books of Joshua and Judges describe ancient Israel's settlement in the land of Canaan. The Book of Joshua describes that settlement as the result of a series of battles fought by a united Israel under the leadership of Joshua. After complete victory over the indigenous population of Canaan, Israel was able to secure its hold on the land and the newly conquered territories were distributed to the victorious tribes. The Book of Judges presents a somewhat different picture. Israel's victories did not neutralize the indigenous population. In fact, Israel's hold on the land was quite precarious. Israel's existence was constantly threatened by its neighbors and the Israelite tribes were marked by not only a lack of a unified response to these threats but also by a kind of internecine warfare that threatened the continued existence of Israel.

The problems of reconciling these two very different descriptions of the settlement period and reconstructing the history of this era are well known. One attempt can be called the "invasion" model. According to this model, the Israelite tribes invaded Canaan toward the end of the 13th century B.C. They engaged in a concerted effort at totally destroying the indigenous population. The invasion began with a campaign in central Palestine followed by later campaigns in the north and the south. These were completed successfully in the space of a few years and the tribes divided up the conquered land among themselves.[2] While this model purports to be based on

---

[2]An historical reconstruction based on this model can be found in John Bright, *A History of Israel*. 3rd ed. (Philadelphia: Westminster, 1981), pp. 105-143.

both the biblical narrative and archaeological data, close examination leads to the conclusion that the supporting data is ambiguous at best.[3]

Another theory is the "immigration" model which describes the settlement as the result of a series of unco-ordinated movements into Canaan by people who come to be known as Israelites from the patriarchal period up to the time of David. The indigenous population of Canaan was never really annihilated by the incoming Israelites since conflicts between the two groups occurred only sporadically. The immigrating Israelites usually managed to live peaceably with the Canaanites until the time of David. David's absorption of the Canaanites into his empire caused a cultural and religious struggle which continued throughout the period of the monarchy.[4] The story of the conquest with its description of Joshua's conflicts with and victories over the Canaanites was simply a tool of propaganda for the Yahwists who objected to the syncretistic tendencies of some in monarchic Israel.[5]

A third model is the revolt model which was first suggested by George Mendenhall.[6] The people later to become known as Israel was actually made up of a considerable number of native Canaanites who revolted against their political leaders by joining forces with an invading group from Transjordan (the Israelites who escaped from slavery in Egypt). This model interprets the available biblical and archaeological evidence from the perspective of anthropology and sociology. It takes into account the socio-economic and political situation of 13th century Canaan and concludes that this area was ripe for revolution. In fact, the Amarna Letters sent by Canaanite

[3]See Marvin L. Chaney, "Ancient Palestinian Peasant Movements and the Formation of Premonarchic Israel," in *Palestine in Transition*, D. N. Freedman and D. F. Graf, eds. (Sheffield, Almond Press, 1983), pp. 44-48.

[4]For an historical reconstruction based on the immigration model see Martin Noth, *The History of Israel*. 2nd ed. (N.Y.: Harper and Row, 1960), pp. 53-84, 141-163.

[5]For a critical evaluation of this model see Chaney, pp. 41-44.

[6]"The Hebrew Conquest of Palestine," *Biblical Archaeologist* 25 (1962) 66 -87. This essay has been reprinted in *The Biblical Archaeologist Reader 3*. E. F. Campbell, Jr. and D. N. Freedman, eds. (Garden City: Doubleday, 1970), pp. 100-120.

vassals to their Egyptian overlords a century earlier describe considerable unrest among the populace.[7] Yahwism then provided the spark that ignited the movement of marginal elements of the Canaanite populace against an unjust and repressive social system.[8]

A growing consensus among historians of ancient Israel is that both the invasion and immigration models are fundamentally flawed and do not provide adequate explanations of how Israel emerged as a separate society in 13th century Canaan. The revolt model does the best job in integrating data from ancient Near Eastern sources, archaeology, and the Bible in its description of how Israel acquired its identity and land. Another advantage of the revolt model is that it provides a sociological analysis of the agrarian situation from which ancient Israel emerged. The value of this model for an understanding of poverty in the Bible is that it shows how ancient Israelite society was formed in the midst of a social revolution against economic and political oppression. The biblical tradition is the memory of a people who emerged out of a conscious and deliberate rejection of an oppressive economic situation. In other words, ancient Israel grew out of a revolt against poverty enforced by a ruling elite upon peasants. It was a revolt against the elite of the Canaanite city-states and their determination to control the peasant farmers. This control did not benefit the peasants but the ruling elite.

The Israelites were those who rejected a socio-economic system based on the oppression of the peasants for the sake of

[7]These letters give a good insight into the conditions in Canaan just prior to and during the emergence of Israel as a separate society. For a translation of some of these letters, see *ANET*, pp. 483-490.

[8]Mendenhall's thesis was developed by Norman K. Gottwald in his *Tribes of Yahweh* (Maryknoll: Orbis, 1979) using anthropological and sociological analysis along with a Marxist hermeneutic. Gottwald's work has attracted quite a bit of attention and positive response from scholars though Mendenhall himself has repudiated Gottwald's approach. See Mendenhall's "Ancient Israel's Hyphenated History," in *Palestine in Transition*, pp. 91-103.

For a discussion of the revolt model from a number of perspectives see *TheJournal for the Study of the Old Testament* 7 (1978). The entire issue of this journal was devoted to a discussion of the revolt model.

the well-being of the elite propertied classes. Along with the rejection of the social and economic order, ancient Israel represented the rejection of a religious system which supported it. Israel's God was one who hears the cries of the poor and takes the side of the oppressed against their oppressors.

Why did the peasants reject the Canaanite social system? What was the reason for their revolt? An unequal relationship between a ruling elite and the peasants is not in itself a sufficient reason for a revolt. If, however, the ruling elite of the Canaanite city-states were not providing a peaceful atmosphere in which the peasants could go about their work, what reason is there to remain loyal to them? The Amarna Letters clearly show that just before the emergence of Israel Canaan was afflicted by all sorts of petty wars between the various city-states of Canaan. How could the peasants work their fields amid this disruption? These wars had just one effect on the peasants: an increase in their economic burdens. These conflicts had to be supported by the peasants and, at the same time, they disrupted their work and productivity. A downward economic spiral was the result of these petty wars.

Another cause of the revolt that gave rise to Israel as society was the taxation which the peasants had to bear. The top-heavy bureaucracy in Canaan extended the resources of the peasants beyond what they could bear.[9] What made this taxation even more hated was that it was seen as supporting "outsiders." Most of the names of the ruling elite in the Canaanite city-states did not have Semitic but Indo-Aryan names.[10] What helped unite the peasants in their opposition was that much of the taxation was probably collective in nature. In other words, the village as a whole was required to meet the demands of the city-state that it was forced to support.

Another more immediate factor that needs to be considered was the contribution of the people who had just escaped from

[9]William F. Albright, "The Amarna Letters from Palestine," in *The Cambridge Ancient History*, 3rd ed. I.E.S. Edwards, N.G.L. Hammond and E. Sollberger, eds. (Cambridge: Cambridge University, 1975), p. 106.

[10]*Ibid.*, pp. 104 and 109.

slavery in Egypt. They showed the peasants of Canaan that it was possible to be successful in a revolt against a powerful military elite. The Exodus group was a living testimony to the power of an oppressed class. Of course, the Exodus group acknowledged that their strength came from their God, Yahweh, who unlike other gods took the side of slaves against their masters. At Sinai, their God was revealed as their only legitimate sovereign and bound the freed slaves to a covenantal bond which provided them with a pattern for just intersocietal relations. What this Yahweh did for the slaves of Egypt could be done again for the peasants of Canaan. In accepting the God of the Exodus group, the peasants of Canaan gave to that God the loyalty which formerly they gave to their human lords. It was Yahweh who was the only source of law which ignores social distinctions in its operation.[11] It was Yahweh to whom taxes were given in the form of tithes. It was Yahweh who led Israel to war. The land belongs to Yahweh (Josh 22:19). This is made clear through the way the land is distributed among the tribes (Josh 13-21). The distribution takes place by lot and since God controls how the lots fall, it is God who distributes the land. The prerogatives of supreme authority were denied to any human being and invested in Yahweh, the non-human lord whose rule the Israelites experienced as liberating.

The Book of Joshua contains remembrances of how the peasants of Canaan were incorporated into the community of those who rejected any human lord and bound themselves to the exclusive service of their non-human Lord, Yahweh. Joshua 3-5 and 24 recapitulate the Exodus and Sinai events and describe ritual activities through which new members came to be included among the people of Yahweh. Their energies are directed at defeating their common enemies. Their

[11]In legal texts from Mesopotamia, social status is taken into account when the crime is evaluated and the penalty assessed. See Moshe Greenberg, "Crimes and Punishments" in *The Interpreter's Dictionary of the Bible.* Vol. 1, p. 737.

Chaney, *op. cit.*, p. 71 lists a number of distinctive features of Israelite law which center on their concern for people of lower social status. He considers this support for the peasant revolt model.

covenant with God and with each other is affirmed and celebrated. These ceremonies took place at Gilgal and Shechem, places easily accessible from the central highlands, which was the area occupied by premonarchic Israel.

One important criticism of this revolt model is that the Bible does not mention it specifically. It is important to remember, however, that the account of Israel's settlement in Canaan, as it stands today, is the product of an era far removed from the events themselves. At the very earliest, these accounts date from the late monarchic period when there probably was not much sympathy for peasant revolts among Israel's own elite. But there are remembrances of such a revolt even in the later reworking of the traditions concerning the settlement. Consider the story of Rahab and the spies in Joshua 2. Rahab represents the urban lower classes. Because she is a prostitute, she is among the debased and expendable elements of the city. The spies are those rural elements who oppose royal authority. When threatened with capture, the spies flee to the hills which provided a safe haven for the revolutionaries. The narrative describes the alliance between the urban and rural revolutionaries. The former want to be sure that the revolution will succeed (Josh 2:9a, 14b, 24a) and that they will survive the conflict (Josh 2:12-14, 18-19). On the other hand, the latter want to be certain that they will not be betrayed to those loyal to the king (Josh 2:14, 20-21). It is clear that Rahab and the spies are in conflict with the king and his servants. Certainly the peasants would have cherished the memory of how one of their own outsmarted the king and made him appear foolish.

The connection of the Rahab story with the narrative of the fall of Jericho is artificial. If the town was to be taken by miraculous means, why send out spies? Since military strategems were not a part of the conquest of Jericho, what is the point of reconnaissance? The description of Jericho's fall in Joshua 6 is a thinly disguised account of the liturgical celebration of the city's fall. One can certainly visualize the peasants of Canaan celebrating their victories by marching around the ruins of Jericho, a symbol of the fall of the ruling elite of Canaan. Later Israel's own ruling elite historicized the ritual into an account of the miraculous defeat of the city even though the tradition preserves the memory of a battle fought over Jericho (Josh 24:11a).

Joshua 9-10 preserves the memory of a covenant between Israel and the Gibeonites and Joshua 24 that of a covenant with the Shechemites. In the century before the emergence of Israel, the area of central Palestine where Gibeon and Shechem were located, was marked by revolutionary activity against the Canaanite political system. The people of these two cities were already disaffected and were ready to join the Israelites in their conflict with the Canaanite lords of the area.[12] The central hill country would no longer be subject to the will of the ruling elite who, however, continued to control the coastal plains and the trade routes.[13]

Narratives in the Book of Judges also give credence to the theory that Israel arose in Canaan as the result of a revolt against oppression. For example, Judges 3:12-30 tell the story of the Benjaminite Ehud who was responsible for transferring the taxes owed by his tribe to Eglon, the king of Moab. Again this story is the kind of self-congratulation that the peasants of Canaan would have loved to retell. It is a coarse Benjaminite saga about one of their own who was able to outwit the king and his soldiers. It came to be appreciated as the story of Israel in microcosm. Similarly the Song of Deborah (Judg 5), which is one of the most ancient texts in the Bible, preserves the memory of a peasant's warfare with the kings of Taanach and Megiddo (Judg 5:19). The kings had the chariot army while the peasants had only their small arms. Normally this would

---

[12]For a more complete discussion of this process of incorporation see Bruce Halpern, "Gibeon: Israelite Diplomacy in the Conquest Era," *Catholic Biblical Quarterly* 37 (1975) 303-316.

[13]Joshua 12 lists cities and their Canaanite rulers who were defeated by Israel. Rather than thinking of the destruction of entire cities and the annihilation of their entire population, we should think that the Israelites were able to withdraw their allegiance from the rulers of these cities. The Israelite tribes then maintained control of the highlands while the Canaanite cities still controlled the coastal plain and the trade routes that did not come under Israelite control until the time of David.

have been a mismatch but when the rains came (Judg 5:20-21), the chariots lost their maneuverability and the kings of Canaan lost their edge. The peasants were victorious.

There is just one instance when a Hebrew term for "the poor" is used in the narratives about the settlement. It comes in the Gideon story (Judg 6-9). The raids of the Midianites against the Israelite settlers in the central highlands of Manasseh were making the plight of those farmers desperate. Their long months of work went for naught since the Midianite bandits took away the harvest of the Israelites. This reduced those farmers to poverty (Judg 6:6).[14] Once again in their poverty the people call to God and God responds to the cry of the poor. God selects Gideon to be the instrument through which the Israelite farmers would find relief. The way the poverty of these farmers is going to be handled is not through the charity of those Israelites who were not touched by the Midianite raids but through the neutralization of those responsible for the oppression.

Gideon states that he belongs to the poorest clan in his tribe (Judg 6:15). The choice of Gideon is not made to idealize poverty as much as it is to show that God's choice does not always fall on the best qualified. Once again we have the picture of peasant farmers trying to defend themselves against people who live by the force of arms. It apparently is another mismatch but in the end Israel is victorious because of God's help. Gideon's qualifications do not matter. Later on in Gideon's story it becomes clear that God's military strategy does not always follow normal patterns (Judg 7:2-9).

The books of Joshua and Judges do not deal with the poor explicitly because Israel is portrayed as a group of escaped slaves from Egypt who provide the catalyst leading the disaffected peasants of Canaan to withdraw their allegiance from their Canaanite overlords. Thus these books present the rise of Israel in Canaan as a struggle against power and

---

[14]The RSV translates Judges 6:6 "And Israel was brought very *low* because of Midian. . . ." The Hebrew word translated as "low" is *dal* whose semantic field includes poverty. The meaning of this verse is that Israel was impoverished by the raids of the Midianites.

wealth. Yahweh is a God who takes the side of slaves and peasants in their conflicts with those who oppress them. The very beginnings of Israel are a struggle for justice. Through their victory over their Canaanite rulers, the people of Yahweh are able to take control over their own destiny by denying to any human power the right to levy taxes, to wage war, to distribute land, to give laws. All these are now the prerogatives of their non-human Lord, Yahweh, who has always saved and protected the poor. Certainly there is no idealization of poverty and oppression here. They are opposed vigorously by Yahweh who champions the cause of the poor against those guilty of oppressing them. Yahweh gives the poor a land where they can direct their own destiny free from allegiance to any human lord.

The Transition to the Monarchy: 1st Samuel

A most significant occurrence of one of the Hebrew words for "poor" comes in Hannah's Song (1 Sam 2:1-10). In its present context this song is a hymn of praise directed at God who gave the child Samuel to the barren Hannah. Hannah considered her inability to have children a deprivation; hence, she uses the word *'oni* (affliction, poverty) to describe it (1 Sam 1:11). To make matters worse Hannah's husband, Elkanah, had another wife named Peninnah who had a number of children and who mocked Hannah because of her barrenness (1 Sam 1:6). Hannah's hymn offers her the opportunity to exult over the frustration of her rival (vv. 1b and 5b).

Hannah's Song had a different setting and function before it came to be placed in its present context. It probably served as a song of thanksgiving in Israel's cult. It originally celebrated a military victory of Israel's king and army. The song speaks of a barren woman who eventually has seven children (v. 5b) while Hannah was the mother of six children (Samuel plus the five others named in 1 Samuel 2:21). The poem is martial in tone and imagery (v. 4) which is not at all appropriate to Hannah's situation. The enemies in the song are warriors and not a rival wife. The song concludes with a prayer for the king (v. 10b) that is an anachronism in Hannah's time since the Israelite monarchy did not even come into existence until her son Samuel was an old man. 1 Samuel 2:11 can follow 1 Samuel 1:28 without any problem, which is another indication that Hannah's Song is an insertion in its present context. Still it is not very hard to appreciate why this hymn of thanksgiving was considered appropriate for Hannah. It does speak about a barren woman being made fruitful and the antagonisms described in verses 1 and 3 could be understood as allusions to Hannah's conflict with Peninnah her rival.

The particular part of the Song which will be the focus of special attention here is verses 6-8:

> 6Yahweh kills and preserves life;
> Yahweh brings people down to Sheol and rescues
> them from it.
> 7Yahweh makes some poor and others rich
> Yahweh humbles, Yahweh exalts.
> 8Yahweh raises from the dust the poor;
> from the dunghill Yahweh raises the needy,
> To seat them with princes
> and make them inherit a glorious throne.
> For to Yahweh belong the pillars of the earth;
> Yahweh has laid the world on them.

Verses 6 and 7 contain a series of four lines in which a negative action by God is followed by a positive action. Verse 8 is an extended description of God's positive action on behalf of the poor. The departure from the pattern of verses 6 and 7 serves to place special emphasis on God's positive action on behalf of the poor described in verse 8. The two preceding verses set up this emphasis by stressing the comprehensiveness of God's rule. It is God who effects the judgment which puts down one and lifts up another.

The town dumps (the dunghills of v. 8) provided sleeping

quarters for the poor by night and a place to beg for charity during the day (see Lam 4:5 and Job 2:8; 30:19). God so reverses the status of the poor that they will shift from sitting in town dumps to sitting with nobility. They will inherit a glorious throne.[15] The last two lines of verse 8 place God's actions on behalf of the poor in the context of God's role as the Creator. Because God is the creator of the earth and giver of its bounty, God has the right to insure that the poor have a share in that bounty. If necessary, God will take specific action to insure just that. The Song of Hannah reflects a basic biblical understanding of who God is and how God acts. The God of Israel is the One who takes the side of the poor so that they can enjoy the full benefits of God's creative work. The text does not call for charity and understanding towards the poor; rather, it proclaims God's actions on their behalf.

Another significant text in 1 Samuel which can shed some light on ancient Israel's understanding of poverty is 1 Samuel 8 which describes the request of the elders for a king, Samuel's reaction to that response and God's instructions to Samuel regarding the elders' petition. The corruption of Samuel's sons, who were judges in Israel, led to a request for a king. Israel's desire for a king is considered tantamount to a rejection of Yahweh. After all, when Israel emerged as an independent social group in Canaan, it rejected monarchy. It denied royal prerogatives to any human lord and ascribed them to Yahweh alone. Now the elders of Israel are, in effect, mounting a counter-revolution. They want a *human* king since they believe that such a king will provide the justice and leadership that were simply not forthcoming from Samuel's corrupt sons (1 Sam 8:1-5).

God granted Israel a king despite the sin involved in requesting one. God, however, tells Samuel to advise the people about the consequences of their choice (1 Sam 8:7-9).

---

[15]The words of v. 8a are virtually identical with those of Psalm 113:7-8. Perhaps these two texts reflect slight variations of a standard formula with which Israelite poets spoke of God's actions on behalf of the poor.

Samuel's warning focuses on the claims that the king would make upon the people (1 Sam 8:10-18). Unfortunately no English translation adequately reflects the play on words between *mishpat* in verses 9 and 11 (which is here translated as "the ways" [of the king]) and other forms derived from the same Hebrew root *shpt* (whose semantic field includes justice, right, judgment, judge) in verses 1, 2, 3, 5, 6, 20. This wordplay involves a rather bitter irony. Certainly the people were right to complain about Samuel's corrupt sons and their perversion of justice. Unfortunately, the "justice" (*mishpat*) of the king will be an ever greater perversion of Israelite tradition. The king would appropriate people and property. He would tax the Israelites and conscript their sons and daughters to serve in his army and to support his lavish lifestyle. Everyone living under the king's brand of "justice" will be nothing more than royal slaves (1 Sam 8:15).[16] Instead of being God's servants, the Israelites would once again be servants of a human master.

In effect, the Israelites are choosing the kind of life they rejected in Egypt and Canaan. Giving absolute authority to a human being turns that person's subjects into slaves and creates poverty. 1 Samuel 12:8-11 reminds Israel of their experience with God as their king. Deliverance always came, yet in the most recent crisis Israel lost confidence and asked for a king (1 Sam 8:12). There is no other way to view the request for a king than as a rejection of the kingship of Yahweh and all that it implied for Israel's social and economic order. The rise of the monarchy was a real counter-revolution which effectively negated most of the achievements of the revolt of the early Israelites against the Canaanites.

---

[16]See Ralph W. Klein, *1 Samuel.* Word Bible Commentary, v. 10. (Waco: Word Books, 1983), p. 78. Klein makes a distinction between a secular and theological critique of the monarchy. The latter first begins in v. 18. What appears as a secular critique in vv. 10-17 is, in fact, quite theological for it involves the giving of what had previously been prerogatives of Yahweh to a human being.

The Reigns of Israel's Kings:
1 Samuel—2 Kings

The biblical narratives about ancient Israel's kings are full of instances of the abuse of royal prerogatives. One such incident takes place in 1 Samuel 18:6-30. Saul's jealousy was aroused by the popular acclaim that David was enjoying because of his military exploits, so Saul settled on a plan to eliminate one who had become a rival for the people's affection and loyalty. Saul decided to give his eldest daughter Merab to David as a wife, but David resisted and she married someone else (1 Sam 18:17-19). Michal, another of Saul's daughters, fell in love with David and this played right into Saul's plans. Again Saul offered his daughter to David but he demurred: "Does it seem to you a little thing to become the king's son-in-law, seeing that I am a poor man and of no repute?" (1 Sam 18:23)

From what follows it is clear that David describes himself as poor because he was not in a position to pay the kind of bride-price which a king would require.[17] Saul fully expected this answer. Instead of asking a monetary price, Saul suggests that David could satisfy his obligations by killing one hundred Philistines (1 Sam 18:25a).[18] An editorial comment within the narrative makes it clear that Saul hoped that David would be killed while carrying out this act of service (v. 25b). Though Saul demanded a bride-price that could not be paid without David subjecting himself to great peril, David carried out the assigned task and married Michal. This story shows how people's economic status

---

[17]The bride-price apparently was paid by the groom to the woman's father. It is mentioned only here and two other times in the Hebrew Bible: in Genesis 34:12 when Shechem asks Jacob to state his bride-price for Dinah and in Exodus 22:16-17 which requires a man to pay a bride-price to the father of a woman he has raped. The text from Genesis implies that the father could set any price he desired.

[18]This is reminiscent of the story about Jacob who also was unable to pay a bride-price for Rachel and instead chose to work seven years in the service of her father Laban (Gen 29:15-30) and the story about Caleb who offered his daughter to whoever would capture the village of Kiriath-sepher (Josh 15:16).

enables them to be easily manipulated by people of means. In this case, the poor individual was able to triumph but every instance of such abuse of power does not turn out this way. Instead of being a protector of the poor, here Saul uses his power to manipulate a poor person.

Having been subjected to such manipulation presumably made David more sensitive to the plight of the poor who are in no position to resist the power of the wealthy. But his experience did not prevent David from abusing his power when he became king. It surfaced at a critical moment and brought his own guilt under public scrutiny. The story of David's abuse of power in the Bathsheba affair is well known (2 Sam 11:1-27). It is interesting that like Saul, David too tried to solve his dilemma by sending someone out on a suicide mission. But unlike Saul's plan, David's worked and Uriah, Bathsheba's husband, was killed in battle (2 Sam 12:14-25). David thought that he saved himself some acute embarrassment by having Uriah killed but Nathan the prophet frustrated David's designs. Nathan approached David with the case of a poor man who was taken advantage of by a wealthy man. Nathan used the same word (*rash*) to describe the abused individual as David had used to describe himself when he said that he was too poor to marry into Saul's family.

Nathan's parable of the ewe lamb (2 Sam 12:1-25) is as strong a protest against royal absolutism as one can find in the Bible. The warnings of Samuel about the abuses of power that would accompany the monarchy were not unfounded. Both of the first two occupants of the throne in Israel were guilty of precisely the kinds of abuses which the prophet foresaw. The people became little more than servants of the king. More than any other group, the poor were the least able to withstand pressures that were brought to bear upon them by the king. While Uriah was not poor by any means, still if he could be abused by a monarch intent on making life easier for himself, what would happen to the poor?

As popular as David may have been during the reign of Saul, his own reign produced the kind of disaffection that engendered at least two revolutions: one led by his own son Absalom (2 Sam 15:1-18:18) and another led by Sheba from the tribe of Benjamin (2 Sam 20:1-22). Both revolutions were put down by David's mercenary army which was made up in large measure of non-Israelites who owed their loyalty to David rather than to the people (2 Sam 20:6-7). Apparently the tribal levies, made up of the militia from the villages of Israel, could not be trusted to put down revolutions with which they may have been in sympathy.

One popular revolution that was successful was the one that broke out following Solomon's death. The glory of Solomon's reign was, in large measure, based on taxation which provided for the king and his court (1 Kgs 4:7-19) and on forced labor which provided the work force for all his building projects (1 Kgs 9:15-22). With prophetic support, Jeroboam, who had been in charge of a portion of the enforced workers, led a revolution against Solomon (1 Kgs 11:26-39). The revolution was not successful and Jeroboam sought and received asylum in Egypt (1 Kgs 11:40); however, the centrifugal forces which were destroying Solomon's kingdom could not be held in check for long. Upon Solomon's death, his son and successor Rehoboam was asked to ease the burdens of the people. His refusal ignited a successful revolution (1 Kgs 12:1-16). Rehoboam was able to count on the loyalty of his own tribe of Judah and that of Benjamin. The rest of the Israelite community followed Jeroboam who established a rival kingdom (1 Kgs 13:25-33).

Revolutions occurred because of the kind of abuse which Samuel spoke of when Israel had first asked for a king. Even though theoretically Israel had rejected the kind of social and economic system which was characteristic of Canaanite city-states, the monarchy was established out of a desire for the kind of security that permanent leadership was thought to provide. It is clear, however, that Israel never really made a perfect accommodation to the monarchy. After the revolution of Jeroboam succeeded, the kingdom of the South remained relatively stable.[19] The Davidic dynasty was firmly established

---

[19]The one exception was the reign of Athaliah who was the daughter of Ahab and Jezebel of the Northern Kingdom. She was the wife of Jehoram, king of the Southern Kingdom. Upon the death of her son Ahaziah, she murdered the remaining male heirs

and presented to the people as divinely willed (2 Sam 7). In the North, however, revolution was always a threat. In the first fifty years of the Northern Kingdom's existence, the occupant of its throne was removed violently three times. The bloody revolution of Jehu against the Omride dynasty (2 Kgs 9-10) had popular and prophetic support because of the economic hardships brought upon the poor during the reign of the Omride kings.

The period when Omri and those who belonged to his dynasty ruled over Israel (876-842) was a time of material prosperity if one is to judge by their building activity at places like Samaria, Jezreel, Megiddo and Hazor. But as was the case with the glories of the Solomonic Empire, the achievements of the Omrides were paid for by the poor. Both textual and archaeological evidence shows that the cleavage between rich and poor was growing ever wider during the Omride period. When times were difficult the poor had to borrow from the rich at very high rates of interest. They were forced to mortgage their land, themselves and even their own children (see 2 Kgs 4:1) to survive. Certainly the great drought of Ahab's reign (1 Kgs 17-18) drove many of the poor peasants into bankruptcy.[20] They lost their land to their wealthy creditors who began amassing the kind of large estates whose existence Amos would criticize some one hundred years later. The case of Ahab and Naboth (1 Kgs 21) was probably not an isolated example but the norm of the way the people of means and the peasants related.

Ahab was married to a princess from Sidon named Jezebel (1 Kgs 16:30-31). She probably knew very little of Israelite tradition and cared for it even less—especially when it hindered

and functioned as the sovereign of Judah for six years until she was deposed by Jehoiada, a priest, who managed to save Joash, a male heir (2 Kgs 11:1-20). Athaliah's *coup* was not a popular revolution. It took place not to ease the burdens of the people but to satisfy her desire for power.

[20]The difficulties that such a drought meant in the lives of the poor is well illustrated by the situation of the widow of Zarephath (2 Kgs 17:8-12). For the widow and her son the long drought meant starvation. There is no reason to think that her situation was unique.

what she believed were the prerogatives she and her husband should enjoy as the sovereigns. This is clear from her behavior in the Naboth incident. Ahab wished to enlarge the vegetable garden near his house. To do this he wished to buy the vineyard of Naboth which abutted his own property. Naboth refused to sell, citing the legal and religious custom which held that ancestral property is to remain a family holding in perpetuity (1 Kgs 21:3; see Lev 25:10, 13-17, 23-24, 34). While Ahab was bitterly disappointed, he probably understood the reason for Naboth's refusal. Jezebel was not so understanding. When she found out the reason for her husband's disappointment, she mockingly asked him: "Do you now govern Israel?" (1 Kgs 21:7). She was asking her husband to act like the king he was. Jezebel, who was not fettered by Israelite tradition which put limits on the sovereign's power, was more than ready to give Ahab an object lesson on royal prerogatives. She arranged with the nobles and elders of Naboth's city to trump up some charges against Naboth.[21] Naboth was found guilty of treason and executed. His property was confiscated by the crown. Ahab was able to plant his vegetables (1 Kgs 21:8-16).

The prophet Elijah could not allow this exercise of raw power to go unchallenged. He confronted Ahab and held him guilty of the judicial murder of Naboth (1 Kgs 21:17-19). Incidents similar to this one were repeated often, especially in times of economic difficulty when peasants had to go into debt simply to survive. Their land was their only possession, and selling it meant that their descendants would be condemned to a life of poverty in an economy that was basically agrarian. The reason for the custom which required ancestral holdings to remain in the family was precisely to avoid creating a permanent poor caste within Israel. The land, which was the basis of prosperity, was always to be the inheritance of all Israel. The prophets saw actions like that of Ahab and Jezebel

---

[21]Jezebel's ability to coopt the citizens of Naboth's own town shows the ability of wealth and power to corrupt. Perhaps these people believed that they were preserving their own position or perhaps enhancing it by cooperating with Jezebel in the prosecution of a man they knew to be innocent.

as a rejection of the divinely established order. It was Yahweh who owned the land according to Israelite theology and it was Yahweh who gave it as an inheritance to *all* Israel. Crimes such as those committed against Naboth not only condemned entire families to poverty but also were a rejection of Yahweh's right as well. The only true sovereign in Israel was Yahweh— not Ahab or any other king. Given the attitudes of people such as Ahab and Jezebel, it is little wonder then that Elisha considered it the divine will that the dynasty of Omri should come to an end. He fomented the revolution of Jehu who saw himself as putting an end to the kind of injustice that consumed Naboth (2 Kgs 9:1-37, especially vv. 21-26).

Although this revolution was a *coup* by Jehu, who was an army commander, the level of violence (see 2 Kgs 9-10) indicates something more. No doubt it was the release of years of pent-up anger and frustration on the part of the people. Not only were the kings of Israel and Judah killed, Jezebel and the entire family and court of Ahab were exterminated. Visitors from the royal court of Judah happened to be in Samaria when the revolution erupted. Though they had nothing to do with the situation in the North, they too were killed. Finally supporters of Jezebel were lured into her temple dedicated to Baal and killed. The temple itself was razed. Jehu's purge was brutal in the extreme. Everyone even remotely connected with the royal house of Omri and all those who supported the dynasty were eliminated. Such a bloodbath cannot be justified from a moral sense, but it does show the depth of alienation that the people felt. They showed no mercy to the royal establishment of the Omrides. Such ferocity can be explained only by long-standing injustice. Israel arose as a protest against an unjust social system. It was folly for Israel's kings to believe that the people would long endure injustice.

Unfortunately the situation in Israel did not improve for the ordinary person. First of all, some believed that Jehu went too far with his purge. A hundred years later, the memory of the purge's ferocity was recalled and condemned: "...for yet a little while and I [the Lord] will punish the house of Jehu for the blood of Jezreel and I will bring an end to the kingdom of the house of Israel" (Hos 1:4). Jehu apparently did not take any effective action against the oppression of the poor. This must have continued as is obvious from the message of Amos. That is the almost inevitable result of institutionalized repression of the poor. When the pressures become so great that violent revolution erupts, the revolution often consumes the very people whose oppression caused it in the first place. These internal problems were compounded by the rise of Syria under Hazael who stripped the Northern Kingdom of quite a lot of its territory during the reigns of Jehu and his son Jehoahaz (2 Kgs 10:32-33; 13:3-7). No doubt the peasantry suffered the most during these military and political disruptions though apparently there was some relief for them (2 Kgs 13:5).

Eventually Israel enjoyed a resurgence of military and economic power. This resurgence was reached under Jeroboam II (784-746). Excavations at Samaria, the capital of the North, revealed that Israel's upper classes lived in unprecedented luxury.[22] But the prophets, Amos and Hosea, make it quite clear that beneath the appearance of well-being, the peasants, the poor, the ordinary folk of Israel suffered in order to provide the wealthy with their high standard of living. Amos portrays a picture of Israelite society which is characterized by obvious injustices and an ever widening gulf between the rich and the poor, for example, the farmers whose survival was dependent upon nature and the moneylenders. Whenever there was a drought or other natural calamity, the farmers were certain to be visited by their creditors who were unmerciful in their dealings with the poor (Amos 4:6-9). The creditors were not satisfied with benefitting from the vagaries of nature but often resorted to all sorts of schemes to wrest land from the poor in order to increase their own holdings (Amos 2:6-7; 5:11; 8:4-6). Since the judicial system was on the side of the wealthy, the poor had no alternative but to watch themselves being stripped of their property, possessions and sometimes even their very persons (Amos 5:10-12).

[22]A. Parrot, *Samaria, the Capital of the Kingdom Israel.* (London: SCM Press, 1958).

The portrait of Israel provided by Amos shows the complete transformation of the Israelite society under the monarchy. Israel began as a society without class distinctions united under the law of the covenant. This is not to say that there were no problems but all controversies were dealt with according to the values and processes of that law. With the monarchy came not only a privileged class but also royal courts which rent the traditional fabric of Israelite society. In spite of protest and even violent revolution, these changes continued unabated until the society was so divided, its strength so depleted, its vitality so sapped that it was easy prey for the Assyrians.

Upon Jeroboam II's death, chaos came to reign in Israel (2 Kgs 15:8-28). Within ten years Israel had five kings, three of whom seized the throne through *coups*. There was a complete collapse of law and order (Hos 4:1-3; 7:1) with the poor suffering the most from Israel's internal disintegration. The prophets also chronicle the breakdown of religious values which should have served to unite the people and forestall what appeared to be the inevitable fall of the kingdom. The disintegration of Israelite society was marked by bitterness, unchecked self-interest and jealousy. The people were turning on one another (Isa 9:19-20). The final step in Israel's march to self-destruction was a fatal miscalculation by King Pekah (737-732) who foolishly joined a coalition of small states against the mighty Assyrian Empire. The Assyrians reduced the once mighty Kingdom of Israel to a tiny vassal state which was allowed to survive as long as it did nothing to irritate the Empire. Israel's last king, Hoshea (732-724), signed the nation's death warrant when he revolted against the Assyrians (2 Kgs 17:1-6). Israel fell in 721. According to Assyrian sources 27,290 Israelites were deported to Upper Mesopotamia and Media. Other deportations followed. These deportees (the so-called Ten Lost Tribes) simply disappear into the pages of history never to be heard from again. The devastated land was repopulated with people from Babylon and elsewhere. These intermarried with the Israelite population which remained in the land. Their descendants were the Samaritans.

Perhaps the Kingdom of Israel would have fallen to the mighty Assyrian Empire under the best of conditions. What made this fall even more tragic was that it was preceded by the total rupture of Israel's unity. The nation was divided into two groups. The first was made up of the king, his court and supporters. The latter believed that their prosperity was an outgrowth of royal policies. The king, hungry for the support of the powerful, allowed them to get away with the grossest of injustices against the peasant class. In fact, as the Naboth incident shows, even royalty was not above judicial murder in order to increase their own holdings. The second group was made up of the peasant farmers whose existence was always precarious. These people were defenseless against the avarice of the people of means who used every mishap suffered by the peasants as well as even legal and illegal means to turn the disadvantages of the poor into advantages for themselves. Israel divided into these two classes could not long survive and it did not.

The Kingdom of Judah survived for 134 years longer than that of Israel. This was not because the social situation was any better there than in the Northern Kingdom. Judah's monarchy was much more stable than that of Israel, with the Davidic dynasty remaining in power from the time of David to the fall of the state. Secondly, Judah's monarchs tended to take a less aggressive stance in international politics than did their counterparts in Israel. The one king, Josiah, whose reign was marked by some attempts to regain the glories of the Davidic Empire, died in the attempt (2 Kgs 23:29-30). There were even some attempts at reform. Though there is not any direct information, the cultic reform of Hezekiah (2 Kgs 18:3-6) must have had some repercussions on the socio-economic level as well. A return to strict Yahwism had to end some of the grosser forms of social injustice. The prophet Isaiah was supportive of Hezekiah (2 Kgs 19:1-37 and 20:1-11). Such support would be unthinkable were the king to be guilty of practicing or condoning oppression of the poor.

Unfortunately Hezekiah's reform was followed by a reversion to religious and moral decay under his son Manasseh and his grandson Amon (2 Kgs 21:1-26). The Bible's condemnation of Manasseh is unprecedented because his reign was perhaps the greatest threat to the integrity of Yahwism ever presented. In the atmosphere where even the pretense of loyalty to the ancestral religion was abandoned, it is no wonder that incidents of violence and injustice multiplied (Zeph 1:9; 3:1-7). What was even more tragic was the view that Yahweh was not able to deal with these injustices (Zeph 1:12). Amon was assassinated (2 Kgs 21:23) by members of the court who probably acted out of their concern regarding the foreign policy of the kingdom. The attachment of Judah to the Davidic dynasty manifested itself when the "people of the land"[23] executed Amon's assassins and installed his son Josiah on the throne of David (1 Kgs 21:22).

Josiah, among his other accomplishments, engineered another religious reform (see 2 Kgs 22-23). Although the Bible concentrates on the cultic aspects of this reform, it is clear that the reform was more wide-ranging. According to the tradition preserved in the Deuteronomistic History, the reform began after a copy of "the Book of the Law" was found in the course of repair work in the Temple (2 Kgs 22:1-20).[24] Although the book is not identified specifically, it is clear that the Deuteronomistic writers want it understood that this book is a copy of the Book of Deuteronomy.[25] Now the Book of Deuteronomy is only minimally concerned with matters of cult and

---

[23]This term occurs frequently in the Bible especially in Jeremiah, Ezekiel, 2 Kings and 2 Chronicles. It probably refers to the leadership of the peasant class in contrast to the ruling class made up of the bureaucrats and other royal retainers. Later this term takes on a pejorative sense (Ezra 10:2, 11; Neh 10:30) as it comes to refer to Jews who did not know nor observe the Law according to the standards set by Ezra and Nehemiah.

[24]The Chronicler's History is somewhat different for it states that the reform was already in progress when the book was found (2 Chr 34:1-33). It is clear then that "the Book of the Law" plays a central role in the Deuteronomistic presentation of Josiah's reform.

[25]The predominant scholarly view also has identified "the Book of the Law" with Deuteronomy or some form of it although there have been some suggestions otherwise. See A.D.H. Mayes, *Deuteronomy*. New Century Bible Commentary. (Grand Rapids: Eerdmans, 1981), pp. 85-103.

ritual. Its basic concern is to motivate its readers to observe traditional Yahwistic moral values, one of which is certainly the need for just intersocietal relationships.

The restoration of a just society was probably not the principal impulse for Josiah's reform. It was probably more a matter of resurgent nationalism after years of humiliation under the Assyrian Empire. But once reform was sweeping through the land, its contours could not be controlled by such a narrow purpose. The atmosphere created by Josiah's reform provided an opportunity for prophets such as Zephaniah and Jeremiah to speak out about the abuse of the poor. Jeremiah especially called for something more than simple cultic reform. He wanted Judah to return to the ancient traditional values of Yahwism (Jer 6:16-21). Unfortunately the zeal for reform ended with the death of Josiah in battle against the Egyptians. In the aftermath of this tragedy, Judah's fate was sealed. It was not long before this kingdom too fell, due to the overwhelming power of a foreign invader. This time it was Babylon. Beginning in 597, there began at least two deportations which sent the leading citizens of Judah to exile in Babylon (2 Kgs 24:10-17; 25:11). In 587, the Temple was destroyed and the Kingdom of Judah was no more.

It is significant that the poor were left to take care of the land after these deportations (2 Kgs 24:14; 25:12). Now they would be finally free of the rapaciousness of the wealthy for the latter found themselves expelled from the land which they schemed and cheated to possess. The Deuteronomistic History thus begins and ends the same way: those without the land received land because of God's own decision. At the beginning of this story, the gift of the land to those without it meant victory and salvation for all Yahweh's people; at the end of the story it meant exile for the wealthy and powerful.

Conclusion

The Deuteronomistic History of Israel tells a very sad and indeed tragic story. What begins with so much promise ends with such great tragedy and despair. At both the beginning and end of the story stand the poor and dispossessed. At the beginning of the story stand the people who escaped slavery in Egypt. With only the promise of land ahead of them, they enter Canaan and join with the disaffected poor of that land to establish a new socio-economic order. It is one without great class distinctions. Its foundation was the service of Yahweh, their non-human Lord who gave Israel its land. It was this Yahweh who gave to every family in Israel its own share of the land which was to be the source of its support. Unfortunately the rest of Israel's history is marked by attempts at subverting the divine decision. The people themselves ask for a monarchy which accelerates this process of subversion. In the end, Israel loses its land because some of its people were not content with their share of Israel's inheritance and sought to accumulate as much as possible for themselves. In the end, only the poor were left in the land while the people of means, power, and position found themselves in exile from the land which was to be Israel's everlasting inheritance.

Select Bibliography

Brueggemann, Walter, *The Land.* Overtures to Biblical Theology. Philadelphia: Fortress, 1977.

Conroy, Charles, M.S.C., *1-2 Samuel, 1-2 Kings.* Old Testament Message, 6. Wilmington: Michael Glazier, 1983.

Freedman, David Noel and Graf, David Frank, eds., *Palestine in Transition.* The Social World of Biblical Antiquity, 2. Sheffield, England: Almond, 1983.

Fretheim, Terence E., *Deuteronomic History.* Interpreting Biblical Texts. Nashville: Abingdon, 1983.

Gottwald, Norman K., *The Tribes of Yahweh.* Maryknoll, NY: Orbis, 1979.

Hoppe, Leslie, O.F.M., *Joshua, Judges.* Old Testament Message, 5. Wilmington: Michael Glazier, 1982.

Mayes, A.D.H., *The Story of Israel between Settlement and Exile.* London: SCM, 1983.

4

The Poor in the Latter Prophets

Introduction

Prophecy is not a phenomenon unique to ancient Israel. It has its parallels in the cultures of the ancient Near East. What stands out in Israelite prophecy is its strong criticism of the monarchy and attendant institutions—especially the judicial system (Amos 5:7; Isa 5:23; Mic 3:9-11; Jer 22:13-17). The objects of scathing criticism were the wealthy landowners and creditors who foreclosed on peasants who had been in possession of their own land. The result of their activities was the concentration of land in the hands of a few and the creation of a great number of landless farmers (Isa 5:8; Mic 2:1-3; Ezek 22:29; Hab 2:5-6). Then there were the traders who exploited their customers (Hos 12:8; Amos 8:5; Mic 6:10-11; Isa 3:14; Jer 5:27). The prophets really believed that poverty was the creation of the rich who oppressed the poor (Amos 3:9; Isa 5:8; Mic 2:1; Hab 2:9; Jer 5:27; Ezek 45:9; Mal 3:5).

The prophets were not economic theorists or simply social critics. What they did was to show Israel the consequences of its behavior from their own understanding of the covenant that bound Israel to God. They did not regard poverty as the result of chance, destiny or laziness. Poverty was simply the creation of the rich who have broken the covenant because of their greed. The wealthy used their abilities and resources not to enhance the community but to support their own purposes. In this way they violated the covenant, they destroyed the unity of Israel and called forth divine judgment.

The Prophets of the Pre-Exilic Period

AMOS

One of the principal motifs in the Book of Amos is the need to protect the poor from exploitation. One particularly odious form of such exploitation involved the perversion of Israel's system of justice: "For I [Yahweh] know how many are your transgressions, and how great are your sins—you who afflict the righteous, who take a bribe, and turn aside the poor in the gate" (Amos 5:12). For the most part, justice was dispensed by the city's elders who sat at the city gate to hear witnesses and pronounce judgment in matters of dispute. The foundation of the system was traditional Israelite moral values, the veracity of witnesses and the honesty of the elders who served as judges. In this verse, Amos condemns the integrity of the witnesses who offer their testimony and the judges who are to decide cases brought to them. He accuses them of accepting bribes. When this happens the innocent are condemned and the guilty set free. The prophet accuses Israel of depriving the poor of their rights. An illustration of how Israel's judicial process was perverted is the Naboth incident in 1 Kings 21.

Of particular interest is how Amos equates the poor with the righteous both in 5:12 and 2:6. The righteous person is one who fulfills the demands of a relationship. Judges and witnesses are righteous when they fulfill their responsibilities with integrity. Judges who dispense justice are to be the righteous above all else. They are to intervene to restore the right to those who have been deprived of it. Judges should decide in the favor of those who are needy and deprived. They are to declare the oppressed to be righteous, i.e., in the right. Since the judges do not do this, the prophet does.

God's righteousness was manifested when Israel was declared in the right against those who enslaved it (Ps 103:6-7). God has always put down those who oppressed Israel (Ps 68). Amos wants to emphasize that what was true about the whole community is true about individual members of that community who are oppressed. God declares that the poor are righteous. Thus for Amos it is not the judges who are in the right but the poor whom they convict out of avarice. They are entitled to have their rights recognized within Israelite society yet this recognition was not forthcoming.[1] Amos 2:6 illustrates how the rights of the poor were not being recognized: "...because they sell the righteous for silver and the needy for a pair of shoes...." The first part of this indictment refers to the corruption of the judicial system; the second part describes how venal Israelite creditors had become. They were willing to enslave the poor for the most trifling of debts. While Israel's traditions permitted slavery as a means to pay off debts, here the prophet castigates Israel for the practice of using slavery to deal with debts that are not very serious.

In 2:7 Amos goes on to generalize that the oppression of the poor and oppressed is a crime that threatens Israel's continued existence. The prophet describes this oppression as trampling "the head of the poor into the dust of the earth." The basis for the prophet's criticism was the conviction that the protection of the poor and powerless was at the very center of ancient Israel's moral traditions. This value is reflected in ancient laws, in the admonitions of Israel's sages, in the sayings of the prophets and in the hymns of Israel's worship. Despite the universal character of this tradition, the wealthy of Amos' day did not hesitate to

[1]A.S. Kapelrud, "New Ideas in Amos," *Vetus Testamentum, Supplement* 15 (1966) 203-204.

ignore it and go about selling the poor into slavery simply to settle a minor debt. Amos 8:6 condemns profiteers who take advantage of the precarious economic position the poor occupy in Israelite society. They stoop to the point of selling the poor food which everyone else rejects.

Perhaps the most dramatic accusation of Amos directed at people of means is found in 4:1: "Hear this word, you cows of Bashan, who are in the mountain of Samaria, who oppress the poor, who crush the needy, who say to their husbands, 'Bring that we may drink!'" Clearly the life-style of people of means was built on the foundation of robbing the poor. This the prophet makes explicit in 5:11: "...you trample upon the poor and take from them exactions of wheat, you have built houses of hewn stone...." In 8:4 the prophet makes it clear that the rich are crushing the poor and killing them.

The prophecy of Amos is an uncompromising attack on the social evils of the 8th century in Israel. The prophet excoriates the wealthy because they seize the land of the poor, because they pervert the traditional legal system which is to protect the poor and because they corrupt the economy for their own benefit.[2] His words describe the actions of the wealthy as heartless and dishonest. The pursuit of luxury on the part of the wealthy was predicated on the oppression of the poor. Unlike his predecessor Elisha a century earlier, Amos calls for no revolution since he believes that Israel was beyond redemption. Of course, anyone who criticizes the powerful and points out that their wealth and position were stolen from the poor will be accused of fomenting revolution as indeed Amos was accused of this (Amos 7:12-13). But he vehemently denies that he is a revolutionary (Amos 7:14-15). The prophet probably thought that revolution was futile since he seems to hold out no hope for the Northern Kingdom. He does appear to offer some on the condition that justice be practiced (5:15), but his prophecy as a whole

---

[2]For an excellent sociological analysis of Amos' criticism of the wealthy see Robert B. Cooke, *Amos Among the Prophets* (Philadelphia: Fortress, 1981), pp. 32-35.

does not show that Amos saw any possibility of any change on Israel's part. What Israel had to look forward to is a terrible day of judgment:

> "Woe to you who desire the day of the Lord![3] Why would you have the day of the Lord? It is darkness, and not light. . . ." (5:18-20)

What is particularly significant about Amos' approach to the issue of poverty is that he sees it as the creation of the rich. While the prophet does equate the poor with the righteous, this does not imply any sort of an idealization of the state of poverty. The poor are righteous not because poverty makes people especially close to God but because the rich have oppressed them and have denied them their rights. The poor are faithful in their covenantal relationships; the rich are not. The object of the prophet's words is not to place the poor in a more lofty position than their rights as Israelites allow. What the prophet wants to do is to make certain that Israel knows the cause of its impending and unavoidable doom. In large measure that doom is inevitable because of the treatment that the poor were receiving. They were being denied their rights as Israelites for the sake of increasing the wealth of the ruling class.

It almost appears as if Amos is describing a class conflict as if he were a contemporary Marxist analyst. For Amos,

---

[3] "The day of the Lord" was a central theme of ancient Israel's prophetic faith. It encapsulated the belief that Yahweh would protect Israel from being destroyed by its enemies. Though these enemies may enjoy temporary power over Israel, on "the day of the Lord" that power will be broken. Here Amos turns this hope against Israel.

The origins of this notion are not clear. The expression occurs almost exclusively in prophetic texts: Isaiah 12:2; 13:6, 9; 22:5; 34:8; Jeremiah 46:10; Ezekiel 7:19; 13:5; 30:3; Joel 1:15; 2:1, 11; 2:31; 3:14; Obadiah 15; Zephaniah 1:7, 14-18; Zechariah 14:1; Malachi 4:5. The only exception is Lamentations 2:22.

What Amos implies is that the people are correct in viewing the Day of the Lord as the time when God will move against God's enemies. What the people fail to realize is that because of their oppression of the poor, they have placed themselves among God's enemies.

however, the poor are not really a "class." The poor are so because they are alone and defenseless. They are not in any way organized in opposition to the rich in some sort of a struggle. On the other hand, Amos sees the rich not as isolated individuals but as a group. They are rich precisely because they are able to marshal the forces at their disposal, especially the judicial system, to undercut the poor and thereby increase their own wealth. Amos does not see some class conflict in all this. According to the prophet, it is clear that Yahweh and Yahweh alone will bring vengeance upon the wealthy.

ISAIAH

Amos preached in the Northern Kingdom but he had a "twin" in the south who delivered the kind of denunciation of social inequities that are remarkably like his own. With anger that bordered on rage, Isaiah rails against the wealthy landowners and corrupt judges whose scruples did not prevent them from conspiring in order to rob the poor of their rights:

> "Your princes are rebels and companions of thieves. Every one loves a bribe and runs after gifts. They do not defend the fatherless, and the widow's cause does not come to them" (1:23);

> "Yahweh enters into judgment with the elders and princes of the people: 'It is you who have devoured the vineyard, the spoil of the poor is in your houses. What do you mean by crushing my people, by grinding the face of the poor?' says the Lord God of hosts" (3:14-15);

> "Woe to those who join house to house, who add field to field until there is no more room, and you are made to dwell alone in the midst of the land" (5:8);

> "Woe to those...who acquit the guilty for a bribe, and deprive the innocent of their rights!" (5:22-23);

> "Woe to those who decree iniquitous decrees, and the writers who keep writing oppression, to turn aside the needy from justice and to rob the poor of my people of their right, that widows may be their spoil and that they may make the fatherless their prey!" (10:1-2)
> "The knaveries of the knave are evil; he devises wicked devices to ruin the poor with lying words, even when the plea of the needy is right." (32:7)

As was the case with Amos, the prophet Isaiah sees poverty as the creation of the wealthy. Poverty is made by the corruption of the judicial system and the avarice of the wealthy. They conspire to deprive the poor of their rights and to confiscate their land in order to make their own immense holdings increase. The decadent people of means are pampered and pleasure-seeking (Isa 3:16-4:1: 5:11-12, 22), and the meager possessions of the poor are one means of support to maintain the life-style of the wealthy. Isaiah believes that he is speaking to people who are unwilling to accept correction. Using a familiar metaphor (5:1-7), the prophet compares the people of Judah to a well-tended vineyard, which should be producing a fine harvest but is not. Such unproductive vineyards are abandoned by their owners to the thorns and briars. The same will be true of Judah. The prophet declares Judah's worship in the Temple unacceptable and even offensive to God because of the many crimes against the poor that were committed by those very people whose "generosity" made worship in the Temple the lavish affair that it was (1:10-17). Finally, like Amos, Isaiah sees the Day of the Lord as a day of judgment (2:6-21). He describes that day as a time of humiliation for the rich (3:16-4:1). The prophet knows that the nation was decaying from within (3:1-12) and was heading for ruin (6:11-12). There would survive an insignificant remnant (10:22-23), but even this remnant would be consumed in a new catastrophe (6:13).

In spite of these harsh words of judgment, Isaiah does not give up on Judah entirely. He believes in a God whose purpose could not be frustrated by the avarice and covetousness of the wealthy. The prophet looks forward to a king from David's dynasty who will fulfill the ideals of the monarchy as celebrated in the cult.[4] The reign of this ideal David will be marked by the triumph of justice and righteousness (9:7; 11:5). Unlike those judges who have perverted the judicial system in favor of the wealthy, the ideal king whom Isaiah hoped for will "not judge by what his eyes see or decide by what his ears hear, but with righteousness he shall judge the poor, and decide with equity for the meek of the earth" (11:3-4). Though the prophet was no doubt devastated by the level of injustice that he saw, he tried to engender the hope that God will bring a renewed people out of the disaster that faced Judah because of injustice and oppression (28:5-6; 37:30-32).

Though Isaiah was bitterly opposed to the policies of the state which supported the deprivation of the poor in favor of the wealthy, he did not call for a revolution. He firmly believed, however, that judgment was coming upon Judah because of the oppression of the poor. The prophet believed that the Assyrian Empire was the instrument of that judgment (5:26-29). Once God's purpose is fulfilled, Judah will be rescued from the Assyrians just as God rescued the ancestors of Israel from Egypt (10:24-27). The message of the prophet appears to be somewhat paradoxical. It was precisely the failure of the monarchy to live up to its obligations that brought Judah to the brink of destruction, yet the prophet sees a renewed monarchy as the divinely chosen means for the reestablishment of justice for the poor. Unfortunately the prophet's vision never became reality. The monarchy never became the instrument of justice that Isaiah hoped it could be.

---

[4]These ideals are set forth clearly in Psalm 72. The king is to judge God's people in righteousness (vv. 1-2). Above all he is to defend the cause of poor by defeating those who oppress the poor (v. 4). As a reward for his administration of justice to the poor, the king receives the nations as an inheritance (vv. 8-11).

What is significant about Isaiah's view of the poor is the explicit identification the prophet makes when he calls the poor "God's people" (see 3:14). Though this identification is not complete nor are its implications developed in Isaiah, there may be here the roots of a later idealization of the poor and poverty. The identification of the poor as "God's" is based on the Israelite belief that every member of the community has someone to stand up for them. For example, the woman has her husband to defend her rights, children have their fathers. Where there is no one to defend the defenseless, the judge and the king are to take this role. When these fail to act on their responsibilities, the poor have only one defender and that is God who always hears their cries and responds to their needs. God will not permit the poor to remain helpless. Still the prophet does not romanticize the poor. In 9:17, Isaiah includes widows and orphans among the evildoers and the godless:

> "Therefore the Lord does not rejoice over their young men and has no compassion on their fatherless and widows; for every one is godless and an evildoer and every mouth speaks folly."

Poverty does not make a person somehow closer to God. It is simply the result of being denied one's rights. Even though Isaiah does not idealize the poor, he still maintains that God takes their side. In one of his visions of the future, the prophet proclaims: "The meek shall obtain fresh joy in the Lord and the poor among people shall exult in the Holy One of Israel" (29:19).

MICAH

Micah was a prophet whose ministry began about the same time as that of Isaiah. He came from a small village in the southwestern part of Judah named Moresheth-gath (Mic 1:1). His prophecy is most representative of the perspectives of the rural conservatives who considered the perverse economic machinations of the rich and powerful in Jerusalem as an abomination. Perhaps this is one reason why Micah speaks so uncompromisingly about Jerusalem's dreadful future (Mic 3:9-12). The prophet considers Jerusalem a center of corruption as evil as Samaria and equally under judgment (1:2-9). What he saw going on in Jerusalem was the dispossession of the poor and their families:

> "Woe to those who devise wickedness.... They covet fields and seize them; and houses, and take them away, they oppress a man and his house.... The women of my people you drive out from their pleasant houses; from their young children you take away my glory forever." (2:1-2, 9)

Of course, this could not take place without the willing cooperation of the judicial system which, unfortunately was forthcoming (3:1-3, 9-11). The prophet speaks about the judicial process as flaying the skin off the poor (3:2). The priesthood, which should have protested this corruption, said nothing because the priests did not want to endanger their own economic status (3:5, 11). When the people of means in Jerusalem heard the prophet's charges, they wanted the prophet silenced: "'Do not preach'—thus they preach—'one should not preach of such things; disgrace will not overtake us'" (2:6). The rich do not want to hear where their pattern of behavior is leading them and the whole of the nation. They are confident that God was with them to protect them from all harm: "Is not the Lord in our midst? No evil shall come upon us" (3:1).

Micah's answer to such folly is that God is entering into a lawsuit against Judah and Jerusalem (6:1-8). God will be the prosecutor, witness and judge. God wants justice (6:8); all that Jerusalem could come up with is a well-functioning cult (6:6-7). When judgment will come, Jerusalem will fall but Judah will be saved through a Davidic prince from Bethlehem who will usher in an era of peace (5:1-5; ET 5:2-6).

Micah's prophecy is so special because it reflects the perspective of peasantry from within. The prophet indicates that the hopes of the poor were not outlandish: "...they shall sit everyone under his vine and under his fig tree, and none shall make them afraid..." (4:4). Those who deny this simple pleasure to the poor stand under divine judgment which is sure to come for God will avenge the crime against the poor.

JEREMIAH

The prophet Jeremiah preached in Jerusalem about one hundred years after Isaiah and Micah.[5] Isaiah was a man of the city who considered the wilderness to be a place of demons and robbers (Isa 13:21; 34:11-15). Jeremiah looked upon Israel's time in the wilderness as a time of fidelity: "...I remember the devotion of your youth, your love as a bride, how you followed me in the wilderness, in a land not sown" (2:2). The prophet did not romanticize the past for its own sake, as if there were something about the wilderness itself that brought Israel closer to God. What Jeremiah no doubt was alluding to here is the purity of Israel's religious system at its outset.

Another example of the prophet's idealization of Israel's past is his commendation of the Rechabites (35:1-19).[6] The

[5]While the following discussion will refer to the texts from the Book of Jeremiah as if they all came from the prophet himself, the origin of this material is a bit more complicated.   While some material has indeed come from the prophet, other texts have come from the disciples of the prophet as well as from Deuteronomistic circles which have edited the book. For the purposes of this study it is not essential to settle the issue of authorship for each of the texts under study. What is clear enough is that the texts which follow represent the views of the Jeremian school of tradition which has preserved the spirit of the prophet.

[6]The Rechabites were a kind of "religious order" in ancient Israel. An analogous group were the Nazirites described in Numbers 6:1-21. The Rechabites derive their name from the father of their founder Jonadab, son of Rechab. They came into existence during the bloody revolution of Jehu and assisted Jehu in his executions (2 Kgs 10:15-28). This group considered the sedentary life somehow to be a threat to a genuine Yahwistic faith. Their life-style was a symbolic return to the wilderness. They lived in tents, were shepherds rather than farmers, they abstained from wine (for symbolic not ascetical reasons).

prophet's kind words directed at this marginal group (35:18-19) showed how much he appreciated their fidelity to their principles in contrast to the infidelity that was so characteristic of the rest of Judah. The Rechabites' devotion to the ways of the wilderness was a living condemnation of the lifestyle of the wealthy who were destroying Judah by their avarice.

Jeremiah was not reveling in a kind of wilderness mysticism but was longing for a time when there was a certain level of equality among the people of Israel. During Israel's trek in the wilderness there could be no schemes to acquire the land of others. There were no conflicts between rich and poor. People lived by the promise of prosperity if they were faithful to the covenant. All this seemed to change once Israel made the land of Canaan its own. The land which was the source of Israel's wealth became an object of contention. Gradually there emerged people who began to amass large tracts of land for themselves. Simultaneously there emerged a growing number of landless peasants who became the poor. The status of the latter was permanent since there was little opportunity for people without land to better their economic status.

Undeniable evidence led the prophet to condemn those responsible for exploiting the poor: "...on your skirts is found the lifeblood of guiltless poor..." (2:34). If the exploiters could simply admit their guilt and begin undoing the damage brought to bear on the poor by their avarice, perhaps there would be some hope. Unfortunately the wealthy have sealed Judah's doom by insisting on their innocence (2:35). Their denial of responsibility makes any rectification of the situation impossible. The prophet spared no words in condemnation of those who take advantage of the powerless:

> "For wicked men are found among my people...they set a trap...their houses are full of treachery; therefore they have become great and rich...they judge not with justice the cause of the fatherless, to make it prosper, and they do not defend the rights of the needy." (Jer 5:26-28)

It is unmistakable here: the rich are oppressors of the poor. It is this oppression which will bring judgment upon Jerusalem (6:6). All that the rich have accumulated will be given over to others; what they stole from the poor will be taken from them (6:12). Even the royal family will lose its position (13:18). This is especially fitting since it was the king's responsibility to defend the rights of the poor.

Jeremiah had no love for the kings during whose reign he preached except for Josiah.[7] In particular, he condemned Jehoiakim for expanding his palace and refusing to pay the workmen for their labor (22:13). Rather than protecting the rights of the poor, the king was actually using his power to steal their labor from them. According to the prophet what makes a king is not the splendor of his palace but his administration of justice. Josiah's memory is blessed precisely because "he judged the cause of the poor and the needy" (22:14-16). Because Jehoiakim has practiced oppression and violence against the poor, his death and burial will be so undignified that they can be compared with those of an ass (22:18-20).[8]

Jeremiah made the king's treatment of the poor a barometer of the king's righteousness (22:15-16). Certainly the king had rights but these were subordinated to his responsiblity for the weak members of Israelite society. The prophet condemned the kind of royal ideology which held that the poor and their property were available for use by the king without any restriction. The king had to remember that oppressing the poor was tantamount to opposing God, for God will deliver the poor from their oppressors: "Sing to the

---

[7]The prophet had little love for the abuses of power which were characteristic of all kings. The memory of the abuse of royal power was certainly strong in Jeremiah's circles. He was a priest from Anathoth (Jer 1:1). This was the village to which Solomon exiled the priest Abiathar, who supported Solomon's half-brother Adonijah in his quest to be David's successor (1 Kgs 2:26). Despite this memory Jeremiah still looked forward to a time when the Davidic dynasty would produce kings who would "execute justice and righteousness in the land" (Jer 33:14-16).

[8]See 2 Kings 24:1-5. This is reminiscent of the death of Jezebel who was responsible for the judicial murder of Naboth. The gruesome details of her death and burial were also foretold by a prophet (see 2 Kgs 9:30-37).

Lord; praise the Lord! For the Lord has delivered the life of the needy from the hand of evildoers" (Jer 20:13).

What was Jeremiah's view of the reform which took place under Josiah? While he admired Josiah (22:15-16), he did not discuss the king's reform directly. Yet there are a number of indications that the prophet had some misgivings about a reform of the cult which did not include a return to ancient Israel's traditional values (6:16-21). Being a priest himself, Jeremiah is especially critical of a clergy that proclaims God's peace to those people whose crimes against the covenant are so obvious (6:13-15; 8:10-12). Above all Jeremiah's sermon given at one of the Temple's gates indicates that the demands of the covenant can become lost behind a well-conducted liturgy (Jer 7:1-15; especially vv. 5-7). Any reform that does not include justice for the poor is at best superficial and at worst hypocritical.

Included in the Book of Jeremiah in its present form are a number of sections which are simply summaries from 2 Kings. In those summaries are the texts which indicate that once the Babylonians conquered Judah and Jerusalem and exiled its citizens only the poor were left behind to care for the land (Jer 39:10; 40:7; 55:15-16). The irony is obvious. The rich who spent so much of their energy in acquiring land from the poor now have to leave that land to the poor who were its rightful owners in the first place.

What is unique in Jeremiah are his laments (11:18-12:26; 15:10-21; 17:14-18; 18:18-23; 20:7-13; 20:14-18). These very emotional laments give Jeremiah's readers an insight into the personal feelings of one called to proclaim God's impending judgment upon Judah and Jerusalem. At the end of his fifth lament, the prophet proclaims his trust in God who delivers the life of the needy from the hand of evildoers (20:13). Thus the prophet identifies himself with the poor and provides a religious connotation to the word for poor used here (*'ebyon*). Still Jeremiah like his prophetic predecessors did not idealize the poor for he recognizes that they too may be as ignorant of the divine will as are the rich. In 5:1-5, the prophet is commanded to look carefully for "one who does justice and seeks the truth." If he finds one, the Lord would not subject Judah to punishment.[9] He begins his search among the poor but finds none there:

> "Then I said, 'These are only the poor, they have no sense; for they do not know the way of the Lord, the law of their God.'" (5:4)

He looks among the wealthy and none is to be found among them either. Again this reinforces the conclusion that God takes the side of the poor not because poverty puts people in a special state of closeness to God but because poverty is unjust and should not exist among the people of God.

HABAKKUK

The prophet Habakkuk was a contemporary of Jeremiah whose activity corresponded with the rise of the Babylonian Empire in the last quarter of the seventh century B.C. The book begins with a lament concerning the success of the wicked (1:2-4). God responds that the Babylonians are being raised up to deal with the wicked (1:5-11).[10] The prophet then acknowledges that indeed the Babylonians are the instrument of God's judgment but that they themselves are guilty of great oppression (1:12-17). God responds a second time that the Babylonians will be destroyed by God's power and those who remain faithful will be preserved (2:1-5). The book concludes with a hymn describing God's appearance to do battle with those arrayed against God (3:1-19).

Though there may be some dispute as to the identification of the "wicked" referred to in the opening lament, it is probable that these were the perverse wealthy people of Judah whom the prophet expected the Babylonians to

---

[9]This is reminiscent of Abraham's compact with God regarding Sodom. See Genesis 18:23-33.

[10]Verse 6 mentions the "Chaldeans" which is the name by which the Bible refers to the Babylonians. Chaldea was the name of the region at the head of the Persian Gulf. Babylon was located in this region.

overthrow before being themselves destroyed by God's power. It is possible to read 2:5 and 2:9 as references to the way the rich appropriated the land of the poor in order to enrich themselves even more. It is interesting to note that in the hymn which celebrates God's victory over the Babylonians, the latter are described as "rejoicing as if to devour the poor in secret" (3:14). Habakkuk is familiar enough with the oppression of the poor in Judah so as to use it as a metaphor to describe the scourge of the Babylonian Empire.

Even though this prophet's center of attention was not upon the poor but on the punishment of the wicked and the Babylonians, it is clear that he too knew and condemned the stealing from the poor for the purpose of further enriching the wealthy. The prophet considered the approaching Babylonian army as the means that God has chosen to judge the people of means who have been guilty of oppressing the poor.

ZEPHANIAH

The prophecy of Zephaniah is unlike those which have been considered up to this point. The superscription of this book (1:1) traces the ancestry of the prophet to Hezekiah and the date of his ministry to the reign of Josiah. That the Hezekiah mentioned in the prophet's genealogy is, in fact, the king who reigned some one hundred years earlier is not certain. There are, however, indications that Zephaniah was looking at Judah's predicament from the perspective of circles more in sympathy with the monarchy. First of all, the text betrays a familiarity with Jerusalem and its court, secondly, the text does not denounce the king personally,[11] and finally, the prophet does not show any real concern for

[11]There are some who date the book to the early years of Josiah's reign when he was still a child and when court officials were still in charge. This may be the reason why the king is not criticized *personally*. See F.C. Fensham, "Zephaniah," *Interpreter's Dictionary of the Bible,* Supplement, p. 984.

the poor.[12] The prophet criticizes Judah primarily for the worship of foreign deities (1:5,9); their assimilation of foreign customs symbolized by the popularity among the ruling class of non-Israelite fashions (1:8) and their indifference to Yahweh (1:12). The one text which criticizes the ethical behavior of the people is 1:9:

> "On that day I will punish every one who leaps over the threshold and those who fill their master's house with violence and fraud."

The first part of this verse, which refers to leaping over the threshold, criticizes a practice which reflects the belief that crossing through the doorway of a house was a "dangerous" activity.[13] The second part seems to imply that it was the servants in a particular house who were responsible for fraud and violence. Earlier prophets warned against the violence perpetrated by the powerful on the powerless. Zephaniah, however, does not absolve the upper classes from their responsibility for Judah's impending fate. In fact, 3:1-5 makes it clear that there is not a single class of leaders who are without fault. The prophet condemns royal officials, judges, prophets and priests without, however, specifying their guilt regarding the poor.

Zephaniah does make use of the vocabulary of poverty in 2:3 and 3:12, however, the words do not refer to the economically and socially dependent persons but to people who recognize their complete dependence upon the Lord.[14]

[12]The invective against the leaders of Jerusalem in 3:1-5 may reflect a concern for the poor although they are not mentioned explicitly. Other prophets criticized the leadership of Judah precisely because of their failure to insure that the poor receive just treatment and because of the crimes of that leadership against the poor.

[13]The origins of this belief are lost in the ancient past but it is still reflected in the custom of carrying a new bride over the threshold. The writer of 1 Samuel 5:1-5 was aware of this custom as it was practiced by the Philistines and tries to give an explanation which is more of an apologetic than an authentic account of the custom's origin.

[14]This is certainly why the Revised Standard Version translates the words in question not as "poor" but as "humble" and "lowly."

While earlier prophets condemned the evil people and corrupt practices which made poverty a reality in Israel and Judah, Zephaniah borrows their vocabulary and reinterprets it. He is not talking about material poverty as an evil but he is speaking about a poverty of spirit as a good. The only way Judah will be able to survive the day of the Lord, which will be a day of wrath, distress and anguish, is to acknowledge its need for divine protection (1:14-15). Since God is the protector of the poor, Judah must act like the poor to enjoy that protection. The prophet does not call for the practice of voluntary poverty, but he is calling the people of Judah to express a kind of faith in Yahweh which is nothing less than abandonment to the divine will and absolute confidence in divine goodness. For the prophet, the word which expresses the ideal relationship of human beings to God is the word "poor." If Judah wants to experience a restoration of its former glory, the people must abandon themselves to God.

Except for the occasion when Jeremiah refers to himself as a "poor man," this is the first time the word "poor" is used by a prophet in a metaphorical sense. Albert Gelin in his classic *The Poor of Yahweh* sees this as a "turning-point in history."[15] While it is true that this prophet does spiritualize poverty, one should not conclude that the biblical tradition now begins to ignore poverty as a social and economic problem, as if the "spiritual" significance of poverty makes concern for the "materialistic" side of the question obsolete as a religious and theological issue. The prophet Zephaniah is less responsible for some sort of "turning-point" than for simply reflecting personal background, his audience and the specific point he was trying to make.

The prophet may have indeed come from the royal family (1:1), but he is convinced that what the monarchy allowed to flourish in Judah is going to bring the nation to a terrible end. He takes up a familiar prophetic image, the Day of the Lord, and proclaims that that day is imminent and that it will be a disaster for Judah (1:14-16). He sees that Judah has

[15]A. Gelin, P.S.S. *The Poor of Yahweh.* (Collegeville: The Liturgical Press, 1964), p. 31.

but one chance to avoid total destruction and that chance involves the leadership of the nation taking on an attitude which has been so characteristic of the poor—absolute confidence in God. This is nothing more than what Isaiah said previously. Zephaniah need not be credited with fore-seeing the ideal Israel for the first time. His contribution lay in his proclaiming that message one more time to the leaders of the nation. Any attempt, however, to extrapolate from his message the beginning of some sort of a tradition which sees poverty as a special form of holiness goes beyond what the text of Zephaniah really says.

The Prophets of the Exilic Period

EZEKIEL

This prophet was a younger contemporary of Jeremiah; however, his ministry took place not in Judah but in Babylon for he was among the people taken to exile in Babylon after Nabuchadnezzar's first victory over Judah in 597 (see 2 Kgs 24:1-17). What this prophet says is that Judah's own behavior was responsible for the tragedies that the people were experiencing and would continue to ex-perience for some time to come. It was not God's failure; rather, it was the people's failure that brought Judah to the point of disaster. From the beginning to the end of his prophecy, Ezekiel interpreted the fall of Jerusalem and the exile as God's judgment upon the nation's sin. It was not only God's doing but it was the way that God chose to vindicate divine justice (14:21-33). Among the kinds of activities the prophet describes as "abominations" (18:10-13), Ezekiel numbers the oppression of "the poor and needy," lending at interest (see Exod 22:25 and Deut 23:20-21) and failure to restore a garment taken in pledge (see Exod 22:25-26 and Deut 24:10-13, 17). The prophet equates these activities with idolatry and considers these capital crimes. In a more positive tone, the prophet lists the works of "the righteous" in 18:6-8. These include giving bread to the hungry, covering the naked with a garment, refusing to lend at interest and executing true justice in the case of disputes. It is clear that Ezekiel considers the oppression of the poor as that which led Judah to the "death" of the exile.

When the prophet speaks to the leadership classes of Judah, he unhesitatingly declares their failures with regard to the poor whose rights they should have protected. The ruling classes were responsible for extortion, seizure of property (robbery), and oppression of the poor and needy (22:25-30). In fact, the prophet asserts that these were the very crimes for which Sodom had to pay the ultimate penalty and claims that this proverbial sinful city was not even as guilty as was Jerusalem (16:48-49). He goes on to say that Samaria, which was destroyed for its sins, appears as righteous when compared to Jerusalem (16:51). The prophet accuses the wealthy again in 22:12 of bribery and extortion. When Ezekiel, then, uses the word "poor," he means the socially, economically and legally deprived person. The prophet judges the oppression of the poor to be an act of perversion and abomination (16:49 and 18:12). In the prophet's vision of the restoration, he specifically warns the royal officials to "put away violence and oppression, and execute justice and righteousness." They are to cease evicting the poor from their land (45:9).

What comes out so clearly in Ezekiel is that poverty and wealth are interconnected phenomena. The ruling classes of Judah were rich because they extorted, robbed and oppressed the poor. For the prophet poverty is not a state of deprivation that comes about by chance or because of the foolishness of the poor. Poverty in Judah came about because of the activities of the wealthy whom the prophet compares unfavorably with the people of Sodom and Samaria—two cities destroyed because of their sinfulness. Poverty then is no accident; it is the consequence of decisions made by the rich to deprive the poor of what little they have. When the prophet begins speaking about restoration, he demands that such activities cease. In the new Jerusalem, justice and righteousness are to replace violence and oppression.

SECOND ISAIAH

Ezekiel spoke to Judah in Exile at the beginning of his stay in Babylon. His purpose was to lead the people to understand what was happening to them and why. Towards the end of the exilic period another prophet began to preach. The prophet who spoke to the exiles in Babylon in the middle of the 6th century has remained nameless though his words are perhaps the most stirring of all the prophetic oracles preserved by ancient Israel. Because the oracles of this anonymous prophet were attached to those of the 8th century Isaiah, he has become known as "Second Isaiah."[16] This prophet's goal was to keep alive the ancestral faith of Israel by announcing that Yahweh was coming to redeem the exile and lead them home.

Second Isaiah spoke of the exile as another Egyptian bondage and wilderness wandering, so he described the coming restoration as a new exodus but one which will be a more dramatic reenactment of the events which made Israel a people (43:16-21; 48:20-21; 52:11-12). More than this, the prophet sees the restoration as the culmination of creation itself (51:9-11). The proper response to God's initiative is trustful surrender to the liberation the Lord will bring. The prophet uses "the poor" as the model for those who are waiting for the Lord's mercy:

> "Sing for joy, O heavens, and exult, O earth; break forth, O mountains, into singing! For Yahweh has comforted Yahweh's people and will have compassion on Yahweh's poor." (49:13)

---

[16]The oracles of the 8th century prophet are found in Isaiah 1-39 while those of the 6th century prophet are in Isaiah 40-55.

The prophet reiterates some of what earlier prophets have said about poverty. God is the provider for the poor and the needy (41:17; 51:21; 54:11). The rich and the wicked are spoken of in a single breath: "And they made his grave with the wicked and with a rich man in his death...(53:9). The prophet does not engage in any overt criticism of the wealthy because he believes that it is his responsibility to comfort his people who have suffered the humiliation of defeat and exile. It is his conviction that Jerusalem has paid double for its crimes (40:1-2). Since it is the prophet's goal to preserve the people's loyalty to their ancestral beliefs, he is more persuasive than threatening. He does not announce divine judgment but proclaims God's forgiveness and the imminence of salvation.

A unique feature of 2nd Isaiah are the Servant Songs (42:1-4; 42:5-7; 49:1-6; 50:4-9; 50:10-11 and 52:13-53:12). These poems have a single theme: the servant suffers and is ignored by the people around him. In the future he will be recognized as God's servant and his mission to restore justice will be completed.[17] With justice restored, all people can look forward to a community which is faithful to the moral, social and religious demands of the covenant. It was Israel's failure to live according to these values that led to defeat and exile. Earlier prophets have consistently pointed to the oppression of the poor as the most blatant example of this failure.

Like Zephaniah, 2nd Isaiah speaks of the poor in a metaphorical sense for the most part. The poor are not necessarily the economically and socially dependent but are those who wait with faith and confidence for the coming day of salvation. Similarly the rich are not those who oppress the poor but those who have abandoned their ancestral faith and rely on themselves to secure their future. For both prophets it appears as if humility (the attitude of those who

[17]A question that still has not been answered to everyone's satisfaction is the identity of the servant. Is the servant an individual or a group? Addressing this problem is not necessary here. Whether an individual or a group—the servants' mission is to establish justice.

take refuge in the Lord) is the only acceptable attitude for the people who are to await their salvation which comes from God.

Prophets of the Postexilic Period

THE SITUATION

The picture which 2nd Isaiah painted of a restored Israel's future was marvelous indeed. Yahweh, the Sovereign Creator and Lord, is on the verge of restoring Israel. This restoration will be more than a physical return to Palestine and a revival of a national state. It will be nothing less than the universal triumph of the divine will. The covenant with Israel will be restored, of course, but in addition Yahweh's rule will extend not only over Israel but over the rest of the nations as well. Unfortunately the restoration did not proceed as 2nd Isaiah described it. Only a minority of exiles even wanted to return to Judah even though the Persian authorities not only permitted the return but actually encouraged it (Ezra 1:2-4). The early years of the restoration were marked by disappointment, frustration and discouragement (see Zech 4:10 which calls this period "the day of small things"). There was a succession of poor agricultural yields (Hag 1:9-11; 2:15-17) which left many of the returnees very poor and without even adequate food and clothing (Hag 1:6).

What compounded the problems of the restoration period was the conflict between those who returned to Palestine and the population which had never been to exile. First of all there were the Samaritans who lived immediately north of Jerusalem. They considered Judah an adjunct to their territory and wanted to be in control of it. They regarded the returnees illegal interlopers and tried to frustrate their plans to rebuild the temple and the city (Ezra 4:1-23).[18] Similarly

[18]The incidents described in this text are difficult to locate chronologically with complete assurance because of the historiographical problems of the Books of Ezra

the people of Judah who did not go into exile certainly regarded the land as their own (Ezek 33:34) and would not have welcomed the returnees and acquiesced to their claims to the land. The returning exiles tended to look upon themselves as the purified remnant of the true Israel and regarded both the Samaritans and the people of Judah who did not go into exile as unclean. There were great tensions among these groups and these tensions may have led to violent confrontations (see Zech 8:10).

Even rebuilding of the Temple was stalled despite the economic aid provided by the Persian government. The prophets Haggai and Zechariah believed it was their mission to encourage the rebuilding of the Temple and the restoration of its cult.[19] Until the Temple was completed the people should expect nothing but difficulties, so both prophets spurred the people to action (Hag 1:1-11; Zech 1:16; 6:15). The prophets assured Judah that once the Temple was completed the Davidic dynasty would be restored and the age of promise would dawn. The Temple was finally completed in 515 some twenty-four years after the first group of exiles returned to Jerusalem, but the hopes voiced by Haggai and Zechariah were not fulfilled. The Davidic dynasty was not restored. The community was ruled by a succession of high priests instead. Certainly the people felt keen disappointment, for the restoration was not taking place as had been expected. The situation in which the restored community found itself also set the scene for the emergence of other prophetic voices known collectively as Third Isaiah.

and Nehemiah, but it is fairly certain that the opposition of the Samaritans began early in the period of the restoration.

[19]Haggai and Zechariah were two prophets of the early restoration period. The former preached in 520 and the later between 520 and 518. Zechariah's oracles are preserved in chapters 1 to 8 of the book. Chapters 9 to 14 are later additions. There is one explicit mention of the poor in these books: Zechariah 7:10. Here the prophet asserts that exploitation of the poor was one of the reasons for Israel's punishment through the exile.

THIRD ISAIAH

The last chapters of the Book of Isaiah (56-66) contain oracles of prophetic voices raised both before and after the rebuilding of the Temple in Jerusalem and reflect a conflict of viewpoints within the Palestinian Jewish community during that time.[20] The conflict between those who regarded themselves as true Yahwists and those whom they regarded as evildoers is reflected especially in the following oracles: 56:9-57:13, 21; 59:2-8; 65:1-16; 66:3-5, 17. Other oracles reflect the mood of the community with regard to the unfulfilled expectations of 2nd Isaiah: ". . . justice is far from us and righteousness does not overtake us; we look for light, and behold, darkness, and for brightness, but we walk in gloom" (59:9). The reason for this gulf between expectation and fulfillment does not lie in God but in the people's guilt (59:1).

The dilemma faced by the community was exactly how this gulf was to be bridged. The priestly party, of course, suggested a special fast and the performance of associated rituals (58:1-2). In response the prophet cries out with the passion of Amos:

> "Is such the fast that I [Yahweh] choose, a day for people to humble themselves? Is it to bow down their heads like rushes and to spread sackcloth and ashes under themselves? Will you call this a fast, and a day acceptable to Yahweh? Is not this the fast that I choose: to loose the bonds of wickedness, to undo the thongs of the yoke, to let the oppressed go free and to break every yoke? Is it not to share your bread with the hungry, and bring the homeless poor into your house; when you see the naked, to cover them, and not to hide yourself from your own flesh?" (58:5-7)

---

[20]See Paul D. Hanson, *The Dawn of Apocalyptic,* for a description of this conflict. Hanson maintains that there developed two social classes in the community. One he calls "hierocratic," a priestly party and the other he calls "visionary" which was made up of the disciples of 2nd Isaiah.

It is clear from this text that once again conditions developed which allowed a privileged few to become wealthy while the majority of the people were reduced to economic dependency through exploitation. The people who called for fast days and prayer are characterized by the prophet as greedy dogs who are concerned only about profit (56:9-12). Like his prophetic predecessors, 3rd Isaiah not only attacks this greed but also the belief that the cult provided an indispensable foundation for Israel's relationship with God. For this prophet, the cult was not the foundation of Israel's life with God; it was rather the ritual expression of it. The foundation of that life was just intersocietal relationships. If these relationships were askew, there was no possibility of a positive relationship with God. There needs to be a kind of correspondence between pity and concern for people. Religious asceticism, the renunciation of food and fashionable clothing, is without value. One can and should be ready to renounce one's well-being for the sake of one's neighbor in need. Third Isaiah is convinced that a right relationship with God depends on the right relationship with one's fellow human beings.

In this context, the famous text quoted by Jesus in Luke 4:14-18 should be interpreted:

> "The Spirit of the Lord God is upon me...to bring good tidings to the poor, the Lord has sent me to bind up the brokenhearted, to proclaim liberty to the captives, and the opening of the prison to those who are bound; to proclaim the year of Yahweh's favor..." (61:1-2)

The immediate context points to material poverty caused by the difficult times of the early years of restoration and the profiteering of the wealthy. This text is a prophetic protest against the conditions within the community which allowed poverty to flourish once again. The prophet appears to have equated poverty with piety:

> "But these are the people to whom I [Yahweh] will look, they that are poor and contrite in spirit and tremble at my word." (66:2)

This does not mean that 3rd Isaiah spiritualizes poverty. In fact, in the prophet's vision of the future, gentiles will be at the disposal of the Israelites to do menial work:

> "Aliens shall stand and feed your flocks, foreigners shall be your plowmen and vinedressers; but you shall be called the priests of the Lord, people shall speak of you as the ministers of our God; you shall eat the wealth of the nations, and in their riches you shall glory." (61:5-6)

Certainly the prophet does not see poverty as the permanent state of the pious. He wants to end poverty—not to raise it to some sort of spiritual plane. The prophet also looks forward to a time when people who worked will enjoy the fruits of their labor: "I will not again give your grain to be food for your enemies..." (62:8).

The oracles of 3rd Isaiah reflect a genuine conflict within the postexilic community—not over different spiritual perceptions but over a just distribution of the few material resources that were available to the community: "'For I the Lord love justice, I hate robbery and wrong; I will faithfully give them their recompense...'" (61:8). That the poor were "humble, meek and pious" was no consolation to them while they were being deprived of what they needed for survival. As was the case with the other prophets, 3rd Isaiah too assumes that poverty just does not happen. It is the result of decisions made by the wealthy to steal from the poor and then mask that theft in a cloak of religiosity. This was vehemently protested by the prophet. He invites the community to wait with him for the year of God's good pleasure when God's own representative will put an end to injustice and oppression (66:1-6).

DEUTERO-ZECHARIAH

Two anonymous collections of sayings have been attached to the Book of Zechariah: chapters 9-11 sometimes called Deutero-Zechariah and chapters 12-14 sometimes called Trito-Zechariah. Some of these texts describe the eschatological warfare of liberation which Israel will fight against its oppressors (9:1-8). The ferocity of the battles described there stands in marked contrast to the portrait of the victorious king of 9:9-10 who comes to Jerusalem "poor and riding on an ass." Here the word "poor" does not refer to someone of dependent social and economic status but it refers to someone who has the attitude of the poor. What makes Jerusalem's coming king "poor" is its complete dependence upon God.

Conclusion

The Israelite belief which saw Yahweh as the protector of the poor supposedly gave rise to a new consideration of poverty as specially entitling a person to God's favor. According to this view, the poor were led to accept their condition by the prophets who speak of "submission in faith, an accepted smallness, a religious humility."[21] While there are indeed a number of prophetic texts which call for an attitude of confidence in God akin to the confidence the poor must have since they can depend upon God alone, it is clear that the prophets of ancient Israel do not idealize poverty as a state of special closeness to God. For the prophets, poverty is an evil created by the wealthy who engage in immoral practices to enrich themselves in land and property. In the process they consume the innocent. The prophets see this as one reason for divine judgment upon Israel. In their visions of a restored Israel, some prophets see

[21]See Augustin George, S.M. "Poverty in the Old Testament," in *Gospel Poverty*, M.D. Guinan, O.F.M., editor (Chicago: Franciscan Herald Press, 1977), p. 17.

an end to the injustice which breeds poverty. If the prophets view the poor in any consistent way it is not as people who are in some way closer to God because of their poverty. The prophets see the poor as victims. They have been victimized by their fellow Israelites in violation of the most fundamental stipulations of the covenant. There is only one legitimate response to this situation and that is protest. Clearly the prophets protest against the people who created the conditions which breed poverty and make it a part of the Israelite social system.

The only way that the Bible can effect social change in the world today is if people once again hear the prophetic protest against poverty and those who cause it. Focusing on isolated texts from certain prophets leads to a spiritualization of poverty which sees the poor person as the true representative of humanity. What is most damaging about such spiritualization is that it leads to an acceptance of poverty and a failure to follow the prophets and protest against the existence of poverty which according to those prophets was a terrible scandal leading to divine judgment upon Israel.

Select Bibliography

Koch, Klaus, *The Prophets*. 2 vols. Philadelphia: Fortress, 1983, 1984.

Lang, Bernhard, *Monotheism and the Prophetic Minority*. The Social World of Biblical Antiquity, 1. Sheffield, England: Almond, 1983.

Ward, James M., *The Prophets*. Interpreting Biblical Texts. Nashville: Abingdon, 1982.

Wilson, Robert R., *Prophecy and Society in Ancient Israel*. Philadelphia: Fortress, 1980.

5

The Poor in the Wisdom Tradition

Introduction: The Authority of Wisdom Texts

The wisdom tradition in ancient Israel differs from the priestly and prophetic traditions in a number of ways. One of the most important of these is the authority the wisdom tradition claims for itself. The texts that come from the priestly tradition claim to be the very words of God, for the most part. This is especially true of the legal material: "Say to all the congregation of the people of Israel, You shall be holy; for I the Lord your God am holy. . .you shall keep my sabbaths: I am the Lord your God" (Lev 19:2-3). Similarly prophetic oracles are often introduced with the formula: "Thus says the Lord. . . " Sometimes they are concluded with a similar formula: ". . .a saying of the Lord." Clearly both the priestly and prophetic traditions claim divine authority for their texts. Even though the Deuteronomic tradition claims to preserve the words of Moses, it makes it clear that Moses is actually reporting the very words of God to Israel, which was fearful of a direct communication with the divine (see Deut 5:22-27). Unlike ancient Israel's priests and prophets, the sages made no such claims for their texts.

The authority of the sages derives from their ability to encapsulate the experience of the past in aesthetically pleasing ways—principally in the proverb. What the sages tried to do was to enable ancient Israel to learn from the experience of its elders so that receptive people could learn how to cope with the problems that inevitably arise in everyone's life. Since these problems are recurrent, why not learn how others have dealt with them? The sources for the texts which the sages produced were folk wisdom. Each generation handed down to its successor ancient Israel's culture, values and patterns of behavior. The ethos of ancient Israelite society was preserved in large measure through folk wisdom which instructed people on relationships between parent and child, husband and wife, on the need for self-control, on the value of work, sobriety, good neighborly relations and many other topics whose purpose was to lead people to happiness in life. Another source for the texts which the sages produced was the wisdom of the court. Here bureaucrats and royal officials were instructed in every aspect of their endeavor from table manners to advising the king. A third source was the school, in which teachers instructed their pupils in the ways of the wise.

What made the words of the wise attractive and thereby authoritative was the skill with which these words were communicated. Since the sages did not claim divine authority for their insights, they could not demand that people accept them willingly or not. They had to persuade people by their artistic skill to recognize the truth of their formulations. Unfortunately this aspect of the sages' achievement is lost to the modern reader almost entirely. For the proverbs and maxims which make up the sages' repertoire were meant to be heard and not read. They are replete with rhetorical devices such as assonance, alliteration, puns, and rhyme which cannot survive translation. Yet it was precisely these rhetorical devices and the skill with which they were employed that attracted people to the words of the wise. The skill of the sages in encapsulating the insights generated by human experience in aesthetically pleasing ways was the single most important source of the sages' authority.

Although the sages may not have claimed divine authority for their insights, it is clear from two prophetic texts (Jer 18:18; Ezek 7:26) that some people in ancient Israel came to consider their words on par with those of priest and prophet. Despite this evidence of their popularity, the sages' words nonetheless still do not represent immutable truths but insights which are valuable but yet relative. These "truths" are not pursued for their own sake as if they represent philosophical axioms but they are learned for the sake of leading people to happiness and fulfillment. They are valuable if they achieve those ends. The sages recognized the relativity of their own insights. Acquiring wisdom was stressed by none as highly as it was by the sages themselves, yet they knew that there are no guarantees in life. The road from thinking out plans to the fulfillment of those plans is a long one. Much can happen which is outside of a person's control. Despite the acquisition of human wisdom there are realities which are beyond human knowledge of calculation. Of course, what is absolutely beyond the calculation of even the most wise are the ways of God (see Prov 16:1, 2, 9; 19:21; 20:24; 21:2, 30). When ancient Israel's sages examined life they had to deal with the realms of extreme insecurity compounded by the action of God which was beyond definition. This experience of the divine as a limiting of their achievements was not as frustrating for the sages as much as it was liberating. It allowed the sages to find assurance for their future not simply in their own efforts as important as these were but in the goodness of the Lord which Israel experienced throughout its life.

This view of the sages' understanding of the authority of their statements and their perception of the relativity of their own insights should guide the contemporary reader of the words of the wise. Their observations should not be understood so much as statements about the immutable order of reality but rather as the results of careful observations about the way "things work." The conclusions which the sages make regarding the way "things work" are always subject to revision. (The Books of Job and Ecclesiastes can be understood as a discussion among the sages about some of the perceptions found in the Book of Proverbs.) Similarly these conclusions must always take into account the action of God which is beyond human calculation.

The Book of Proverbs

The modern reader of the Book of Proverbs is usually put off by the Book's apparent lack of organization. While there well may have been an overall conception of the book's composition by the author who put the book into its present form, the Book of Proverbs does not treat poverty and the poor or any other topic for that matter in a systematic way. This should give any reader today reason to pause in the attempt to understand the approach of Proverbs regarding the poor. While it is not impossible to present a systematic treatment of this issue, we have to remember that it is the result of our attempts at understanding rather than of the sages' own work. It is possible to extract from Proverbs some idea of the sages' attitude towards the question of poverty and the poor, yet we need to remember that the Book of Proverbs does not contain a comprehensive and systematic treatment of the question.

THE ORIGIN OF POVERTY

The Deuteronomic tradition presents poverty as the result of Israel's disobedience. If people would obey the law, there would be no poverty. The prophets see poverty as the result of the greed and avarice of the wealthy. The sages, however, approach the origins of poverty from a somewhat different angle. There are a number of texts in Proverbs which present poverty as one consequence of idleness and negligence on the part of the person suffering in poverty:

"A slack hand causes poverty..." (10:4)
"Love not sleep, lest you come to poverty..." (20:13)
"They who love pleasure will be poor; they who love wine and oil will not be rich." (21:17)

The sages were convinced that people were in control of their own destiny for the most part. The choices that they make determine their lot in life. Numerous sayings in the Book of Proverbs denounce both drunkenness and laziness as the cause of so much human suffering. If people neglect their responsibilities because of sloth and excessive use of wine, what other result can they expect but poverty? Success and happiness are the result of a disciplined life according to the sages. If one remains undisciplined, poverty is the inevitable consequence:

"A little sleep, a little slumber, a little folding of the hands to rest, and poverty will come upon you like a vagabond, and want like an armed man." (6:10-11)

Clearly the sages do not idealize poverty or the poor. They recognize that it is sometimes the case that people "choose" poverty, albeit somewhat indirectly. The purpose of the sages is not to castigate such people but to warn the young about the consequences of some of the choices that they will be making. The sages were convinced that actions have consequences; furthermore, the consequences are quite predictable. If experience has taught people anything it is that poverty comes inevitably to those whose undisciplined life is marked by drunkenness and laziness. This, of course, does not mean that every poor person must be an undisciplined alcoholic. The sages are not trying to explain the origins of poverty as much as they are trying to describe the consequences of a life-style that is without self-control. Sometimes interpreters of Proverbs have viewed the sages' observations regarding the connection between sloth and poverty as evidence of an elitist ethic. It appears as if the people who have "made it" are castigating those who have not. In reality, the sages are issuing a warning to the next generation so that the young may avoid the kind of poverty that comes from a lack of self-discipline. They say as much in 13:18:

> "Poverty and disgrace come to those who ignore instruction, but they who heed reproof are honored."

The sages are not advising the poor to "pick themselves up by their bootstraps"; they are warning the young to avoid the kind of life-style that inevitably leads to poverty and disgrace. The sages underscore this advice when they point out that the poor are despised even by those who should be most sympathetic to them:

> "All a poor man's brothers hate him; how much more do his friends go far from him!" (19:7)

Perhaps the reason for this rejection is the knowledge that the entire situation was avoidable. Behind Proverbs 19:7 is the assumption that the poor man chooses his own lot. By leading a dissipated life, a person chooses to be poor. Such an approach to life cannot possibly bring admiration but only derision (14:20).

REACTION TO POVERTY

Though the sages looked upon poverty as one result of an undisciplined style of life, it is clear that this does not represent the totality of their reflections upon poverty. If poverty were, in fact, purely and simply the consequences of the way some people chose to live, it would be hard to see how the sages could come to the point of sympathy for the poor. The sages are, in fact, compassionate toward the poor:

> "They who close their ears to the cry of the poor will themselves cry out and not be heard." (21:13)

They state that justice towards the poor is a fundamental duty of the king:

> "If a king judged the poor with equity, his throne will be established forever."(29:14)

In this regard, the sages followed the lead of their ancient Near Eastern counterparts who looked upon concern for the poor as one of the principal responsibilities of monarchs. Ancient Israel's sages extended this duty to all of Israel. Concern for the poor is a religious duty that is incumbent upon all. In fact, kindness to the poor is considered to be a kindness done to God:

> "They who are kind to the poor lend to the Lord, and the Lord will repay them for their deeds." (19:17)

This text anticipates the teaching of Jesus in Matthew 25:31-40 in which the kindness shown to one in need is equated with kindness shown to the Lord. Similarly the sages equate rejection of the poor with rejection of God (see Matt 25:41-45):

> "They who mock the poor insult their Maker. . . . " (17:5; see also 14:31)

Finally the sages recognize that God is the defender of the poor. Any crimes against the poor call for divine retribution:

> "Do not rob the poor, because they are poor, or curse the afflicted at the gate; for the Lord will plead their cause and despoil of life those who despoil them." (22:22-23)

This is as strong an identification of the cause of the poor with God as one finds in the biblical tradition. Yet these perspectives come not simply from ancient Israel's religious traditions but represent a consistent teaching of ancient Near Eastern sages in general. Proverbs 22:22-23 comes from a section of the book (22:17-24:22) which found much of its inspiration from an Egyptian wisdom text, the *Instruction of Amen-em-opet*. In this text as well, the moon-god Thoth, the jurist among the gods, is described as pleading the cause of the poor against their oppressors. More than any other text, Proverbs 22:22-23 shows that the sages did not despise the poor. They certainly had nothing good to say about those individuals who chose poverty for themselves because of the foolish life-style decisions that they made; nevertheless, they recognized that this folly did not make the poor fair game for oppression. Whatever one may think about the poor, it remains true that God is their protector who regards every act of oppression against them as a personal insult.

THE DESIRE FOR WEALTH

Very often the sages are presented as those who sought success, prosperity and happiness. In a sense that is true, though it is perhaps better to say that the sages were those who sought to find effective ways to cope with the problems of life rather than those who sought to find the solution to those problems in wealth and success. They were realistic enough to know that wealth brought its own set of problems as did poverty. Just as they did not idealize the poor, the sages did not idolize the rich:

> "The poor and the oppressor meet together; the Lord gives light to the eyes of both." (29:13)

The sages prayed that the Lord would protect them from the pitfalls that come with both poverty *and* wealth:

> "Two things I ask of you; deny them not to me before I die: Remove far from me falsehood and lying; give me *neither poverty nor riches;* feed me with the food that is needful for me, lest I be full, and deny thee, and say, 'Who is the Lord?' or lest I be poor, and steal, and profane the name of my God." (30:7-9)

Wealth can blind people to the real source of their prosperity. They can believe that it is the result of their own effective planning and careful judgments when, in fact, it is due to the goodness of God:

> "Many are the plans of the human mind, but it is the purpose of the Lord that will be established." (19:21)

Similarly the privations of poverty can lead people to take the kind of drastic steps that lead them away from God. That is why true wisdom asks for what is necessary for survival. Poverty and wealth are the kinds of extremes that are dangerous because they can lead people to be forgetful of God.

CONCLUSION

The Book of Proverbs closes with a poem supposedly on the ideal wife (31:10-31). It has been suggested that this poem actually describes wisdom to whom the sage is "married" after becoming imbued with the ethos of wisdom as found in the rest of the book. One of the virtues of the ideal wife (i.e. wisdom) is that she "opens her hand to the poor and reaches out her hands to the needy" (31:20). Thus the Book of Proverbs closes with a text which presents generosity towards the poor as the kind of behavior that reflects true wisdom. No matter what may be the reason for a person's poverty, generosity towards the poor is the response that ought to come from the genuine sage.

The Book of Job

Although the Book of Proverbs presents a balanced view of poverty, still its perspectives have been misunderstood and caricatured. Some have looked upon the perspective of this book as eudaemonism overlaid with a very thin veneer of Yahwism. With regard to poverty, the book's teachings have been reduced to simply this: riches are a blessing and therefore poverty must be a curse and furthermore it is a curse which people bring down on themselves. The Book of Job is a protest against such an analysis of the wisdom tradition.

The book is made up of a narrative about an innocent man who endures every sort of suffering without losing faith in God. This man in the end is rewarded by God for his fidelity by having his health, wealth and family restored to him. Between the part of the story which tells about the man's affliction and that which describes his reward there is a very long poetic section made up of speeches made by the friends of Job who tell him that there is no suffering without sin. Then there are speeches by Job himself who says that what the friends say may be theoretically valid but his case must be an exception for he is suffering terribly without any apparent cause. Job challenges God to prove him wrong. Finally God does answer Job by telling him that he is incapable of understanding the ways of God.

One of Job's friends, Eliphaz, states the traditional doctrine that God saves the poor and gives them reason to hope:

> "But God saves the fatherless from their mouth, the needy from the hand of the mighty. So the poor have hope, and injustice shuts her mouth." (5:15-16)

Later on in the book a fourth man, Elihu, speaks to Job and makes essentially the same point (34:19, 28; 36:6, 15) regarding God's care for the poor and afflicted.[1] The ways of God are ultimately just. If Job were just, then he would not be suffering. Since sin and suffering are connected, according to the friends, Job must have sinned. To find relief from God Job must confess his guilt. Job is conscious of no guilt so he asks his friends and God to justify his suffering. Zophar,

---

[1] Some scholars consider the speeches of Elihu to be interpolations designed to provide the Book of Job with a more satisfying answer to the problems which it probes. See Marvin Pope, *Job*, Anchor Bible, 15. (Garden City: Doubleday, 1965), pp. xxvii-xxviii.

another friend, compared the ways of the righteous with those of the sinner. The righteous "seek the favor of the poor and...give back his wealth" (30:10) while sinners have "crushed and abandoned the poor and...seized a house which they did not build" (30:19). Zophar implies that Job may have failed in the area of proper concern for the poor.

In the course of his argumentation with his friends, Job uses a variety of approaches in his attempts to take exception to the doctrine of "no suffering without sin." In 24:1-14 he supports his position by pointing to what happens to the poor and the needy. Job's speech is an indictment of the way people of means treat the working class and make them poor. There is a whole litany of economic crimes: people are cheated out of their land and livestock (v. 2); even the animals of the orphan and widow are taken (v. 3); the poor have to go into hiding to save themselves from physical abuse (v. 4); they are reduced to hunting and gleaning in order to feed their children (v. 5-6); the poor do not have adequate clothing or housing (vv. 7-8, 10); the rich do not hesitate, therefore, to take the infants of the poor as collateral for loans (v. 9). Although it is not the author's intention to provide a socio-economic analysis of Israelite society, it is impossible that these verses are a fabrication of the author's imagination. Job's argument would lack all cogency if these kinds of situations did not exist. The plight of the poor, according to the argument, is completely undeserved and so Job wonders why God does nothing about their oppression. The crimes he describes are committed against the defenseless of society—precisely the people who supposedly were to be protected by God in a special way. God does nothing to defend the poor from exploitation so their confidence in God must be unfounded.

Another approach that Job takes in his own defense is more positive. Instead of accusing God for neglecting the poor and the needy, Job asserts that he has done all that he could to alleviate their plight (29:12-20). Though Job was quite prosperous, he was not uncaring toward the poor. In fact, he was their champion in every way. He responded to their pleas for help (29:12), he helped the handicapped (29:15), he was a comfort to widows (29:13b). Job calls himself "a father to the poor" (29:16). He describes how he went so far as to search out the causes of people he did not know and prevented the unrighteous from expropriating their property (29:16b-17). Job presents to us a portrait of a person of means who uses his power and wealth not to harm the poor but to protect them from the unrighteous. Though Job states that he sympathized with the poor (30:25), his compassion was not a matter of feelings alone. He is quite explicit about the specific actions he took on behalf of the poor. While Job uses this flattering self-portrait of his actions on behalf of the poor, it provides the reader with a model of the kind of behavior which the prophets called for and which they found completely lacking in Israel. They would say that Israel fell because there were not enough people who acted as justly toward the poor as did Job.

To convince God and his friends of his innocence, Job engages in another review of this past (31:1-40). This chapter is made up of sixteen oaths which Job takes regarding different aspects of his moral and religious behavior.[2] As part of his confession of innocence Job asserts that he did not withhold anything from the poor, that he cared for widows, that he shared his food with orphans, and has given clothing to those in need of it (31:16-21). In short, Job calls for vindication by God because he has fulfilled his responsibilities to the poor. Job asserts that he has been more than just—he has responded to the every need of the poor. Job challenges God to prove him wrong and show what aspect of his life shows moral failures. Certainly it cannot be in the area of concern for the poor.

The Book of Job offers a bleak picture of what the poor could expect from their oppressors. Job also describes what

---

[2]This chapter has a number of parallels with the negative confession described in chapter 125 of the Egyptian Book of the Dead. In that text the deceased are required to assert that they have avoided all forms of immoral behavior. If the deceased are judged to be speaking the truth, they are permitted to continue their journey to the other world.

kind of treatment they should receive from people of means. Though the book is not directly concerned with poverty, it indirectly affirms that poverty is caused by oppression. It is the result of actions that the wealthy take—not by actions that the poor do or do not take. They are not masters of their own fate. Also the book affirms that it is the responsibility of the wealthy to take action for the benefit of the poor. This will be one area regarding which they will be judged by God.

The Book of Ecclesiastes (Qoheleth)

Like the Book of Job, Ecclesiastes is a text which is critical of a simplistic understanding of the perspectives which are behind the wisdom tradition—especially as it is found in the more conventional exponents of that tradition such as the Book of Proverbs. Though the author was himself a teacher and collector of proverbs (12:9), he goes to great lengths in order to demonstrate the relativity of the insights of the wisdom tradition. Though the book purports to be the reflections of Solomon (1:1), it was certainly written centuries after that king and represents the reflections of one steeped in the wisdom tradition but one whose experience leads him to question some of the claims regarding the value of wisdom. In fact, Ecclesiastes is rather skeptical about any attempt to find meaning, value and purpose in life (1:16-18). The best that a person can do is enjoy life as far as that is possible (9:7-10). Though the book does not deal with poverty in any systematic way nor is poverty one of the principal concerns of the book,[3] there are a few texts in this book which will help fill out a profile of poverty in the biblical tradition.

---

[3]The tone of the book makes it probable that it reflects the experience of someone who was reasonably well to do. Words such as "profit" and "gain" keep recurring in it. Yet it is clear that the author did not find ultimate value and purpose in wealth.

Ecclesiastes offers another confirmation of the corruption of Israel's judicial system:

> "If you see in a province the poor oppressed and justice and right violently taken away, do not be amazed at the matter; for the high official is watched by a higher, and there are yet higher ones over them." (5:8)

It is clear that the author considered official corruption endemic in ancient Israel. In fact, the very system which was to protect the poor has been perverted to disenfranchise them. Unlike the prophets, Ecclesiastes calls for no revolution, he makes no protest. He simply advises his readers not to be surprised. It is difficult to know whether Ecclesiastes is being ironic or just cynical here when he asserts in an almost offhanded way that oppression of the poor, which is to be prevented by the government is actually promoted by a hierarchy of officials who are in collusion to defraud the poor.

Another interesting insight into the status of the poor is given in a short parable which Ecclesiastes tells:

> "There was a little city with few people in it; and a great king came against it and besieged it, building great siegeworks against it. But there was found in it a poor wise man and he by his wisdom delivered the city. Yet no one remembered that poor man. But I say that wisdom is better than might, though the poor man's wisdom is despised and his words are not heeded." (9:14-16).

This story shows the effects of a social system based on economic distinctions. Even when a poor person does something quite out of the ordinary, he is forgotten because poor people are not supposed to distinguish themselves—or at least that is what the wealthy tell themselves to rationalize poverty. The poor man is trapped; he cannot extricate himself from his poverty by saving his city. Even wisdom does not help the poor man, for the sage who lacks wealth goes unremembered. This little story can help people of means understand how trapped the poor feel. No achievement of theirs no matter how great can bring them out of their poverty. Despite this, Ecclesiastes still believes that poverty and wisdom are better than wealth and position when they are joined to folly (4:13).

Finally in 5:10-6:9, Ecclesiastes points out the foolishness of greed. He begins by asserting that the lust for wealth can never really be satisfied. The more money one has the more money one spends and the more money one needs. Ecclesiastes goes on to describe the loss of wealth in bad business ventures which deprives one's children of their inheritance. But he also points out the futility of working and saving one's entire life just to pass one's wealth on to others. For Ecclesiastes diligence and thrift are simply subtle forms of greed. There are really no advantages to a life of greed (6:7-9). Without words of judgment and condemnation like the prophets, Ecclesiastes just as effectively points out the folly of greed which has moved so many to rob from the poor.

The other side of an insatiable desire for wealth is the subjection of the poor. Ecclesiastes saw what evil resulted from the avarice of the wealthy:

> "And I went round and saw all the oppressions that are practiced under the sun. And behold, the tears of the oppressed, and they had no one to comfort them! On the side of their oppressors there was power, and there was no one to comfort them." (4:1)

This is as touching a description of the lot of the poor as one can find in the Bible.

Ecclesiastes' words give an insight into the social situation of his day, which was probably in the third century. Evidently it was a time when people were engaged in a fearsome struggle for wealth. Unfortunately Ecclesiastes does not give quite enough information about this struggle. He does not focus on the issue of poverty and its associated socio-economic problems. These are merely illustrations of his main thesis: the vanity, the futility of the human situation.

The Book of Sirach (Ben Sira, Ecclesiasticus)

INTRODUCTION

Ecclesiastes is clearly critical of the kind of conventional wisdom that is found in the Book of Proverbs while Sirach stands in line with that type of wisdom teaching. There is, however, a definite polemical tone to the book. The author of Ecclesiasticus is reacting to a Hellenistic life-style and patterns of thought that were penetrating especially into the Jewish upper class.[4] Sirach marshals ancient Israelite wisdom tradition to combat what he considered to be a dangerous development.

The Greeks under Alexander the Great conquered Palestine in the 4th century. The Book of Sirach was written about 180 B.C. By that date, there was ample opportunity for Greek culture to make inroads into traditional Jewish thought and practice. This, of course, was Alexander's dream—that the best of Greek culture be combined with the best of Eastern culture. For some Jews, however, this dream was more of a nightmare because they considered Hellenism a threat to their ancestral religion. One consequence of this attempt to wed the Greek and Jewish cultures was the rise of social conflict among the Jews. On the one side was the relatively small, but wealthy upper class; on the other was the much larger group which was much more conservative theologically and culturally. The former had more dealings with their Greek masters and the nearby states which had

---

[4]The author witnessed this firsthand since he was certainly from the upper class. He states that he held an important position in Jerusalem society (39:4) and that he travelled abroad frequently (34:12). He was a professional man and proud of his position (39:1). Since he attests that he had sufficient leisure time to study the Bible (Prologue 7-11; 39:1-3), it is certain that he did not belong to the peasant class.

also begun to accept Hellenistic ways. The conservatives were not really *one* group but were made up of the lower ranks of the clergy whose attitude is reflected in the Books of Chronicles, Ezra and Nehemiah, those who considered themselves the heirs of the prophetic tradition and those who were giving birth to the apocalyptic tradition. What united these disparate conservative groups was their distaste for any accommodation with Hellenism and their marginal economic status. They saw any accommodation with the Greeks as the product of a desire to win the favor of their foreign overlords by compromising traditional values.[5] Sirach represents those who wished to present ancient Israel's wisdom tradition as a tool to withstand the temptation to abandon the ancestral religion of the Jews through accommodation with Hellenism.

It is important to remember the author's background as well as that of his intended audience. Sirach is the product of an upper class individual who wished to communicate to others of his social class what he had learned from his experience.[6] The purpose of his writing was to insure that his readers would not be so mesmerized by the allurement of Hellenistic culture that they would come to regard their own Jewish culture as an outmoded relic of the past. In his treatment of poverty and the poor, Sirach, for the most part, reaffirms the perspectives of traditional Israelite wisdom but he also includes insights of the prophetic tradition to counteract Hellenistic views which were not sympathetic to the poor. The Greeks did not recognize any responsibility to the poor, while Near Eastern and Israelite tradition always held that people of means are to respond to the cries of the poor, because God is their protector.[7]

[5]The stories about Daniel and his friends in Daniel 1-6 come from this period and reflect what kinds of temptations existed for gifted Jews to compromise their traditions in order to win the favor of their foreign masters.

[6]George W.E. Nickelsburg, *Jewish Literature Between the Bible and the Mishnah.* (Philadelphia: Fortress, 1981), p. 56.

[7]Martin Hengel, *Judaism and Hellenism.* (Philadelphia: Fortress, 1974), vol. 1, p. 48. See also note 381, vol. 2, p. 38.

THE ORIGIN OF POVERTY

Sirach reflects the traditional view of ancient Israel's sages that poverty could be brought on oneself, but the author does not dwell on this point. He is content to warn the wealthy that unless they take proper precautions, they can lose their wealth:

> "Do not revel in great luxury, lest you become impoverished by its expense. Do not become a beggar by feasting with borrowed money, when you have nothing in your purse." (18:32-33; see also 25:3 and 31:4)

Sirach spends more of his energy on trying to make his readers see the suffering of the poor and their responsibility to respond to it. In fact, at times his criticism of the wealthy is quite similar to that of the prophets. In a sense, that is to be expected of a person who saw himself as a successor to the prophets: "I will again pour out teaching like prophecy, and leave it to all future generations" (24:33).

CRITICISM OF THE RICH

The author engages in a very striking polemic against a hectic concern for earning money:

> "A merchant can hardly keep from wrongdoing, and a tradesman will not be declared innocent of sin. Many have committed sin for a trifle, and whoever seeks to get rich will avert his eyes. As a stake is driven firmly into a fissure between stones, so sin is wedged in between selling and buying. If a man is not steadfast and zealous in the fear of the Lord, his house will be quickly overthrown." (26:29-27:3)

The author probably considered traditional agricultural pursuits to be the more acceptable way of earning a living (7:15; 20:28). He evidently had a problem with the emerging merchant class that certainly had more occasion to deal with Hellenists and to compromise Yahwistic traditions than those who followed agrarian occupations. More serious is the author's intimation that the rich take advantage of the poor to enrich themselves. He condemns those who use what they have taken from the poor as a sacrifice, those who deprive the poor of their most basic needs and those who withhold the wages of the poor (34:20-22). He graphically describes how the poor are at the mercy of the rich: "Wild asses in the wilderness are the prey of lions; likewise the poor are pastures for the rich" (13:19).

The words of Sirach point to a social climate that was marked by observable social conflict between the rich and poor: "What peace is there between a hyena and a dog? And what peace between a rich man and a poor man?" (13:18; see also 13:20). What made this conflict so acute was the perception by the poor and those who sympathized with them like Sirach that the rich were ready to compromise traditional values for economic and social gain. The author points to the unequal treatment that the poor had to endure in society (13:3, 21-23) and urges his readers to respect the poor person who fears God (10:21-23). Sirach also notes the penchant the rich had for exploiting the poor (13:4a). The familial ethos of Israelite society as envisioned by the Deuteronomists was certainly not operative in Sirach's day. That is precisely why Sirach engages in the level of social criticism that he does. He encourages his readers to pay attention to what the poor have to say and to treat them with respect (4:8). Despite the social conflict which marked Sirach's experience, he did not condemn riches as such. He values wealth that has been gained honestly because it guarantees a secure life (10:27; 13:24a; 40:18a). But Sirach also warns against the dangers of riches (8:2; 13:15-24). He advises the wealthy to respond to the cries of the poor: "Incline your ear to the poor, and answer him peaceably and gently (4:8; see also 4:1-5; 29:8-9). The motive that Sirach offers is the fear of divine retribution: "if in bitterness of soul he [the poor person] calls down a curse upon you, his

Creator will hear his prayer" (4:6b; see also 7:32; 10:14; 11:21; 21:5; 22:23).

Time and again Sirach returns to the topic of wealth. He compares generosity and niggardliness (14:3-8). He calls people of means to be generous with their help to the needy (4:4-6; 7:32-36; 29:9-13). Because the poor need loans to survive at times, he asks the wealthy to be forthcoming even though there are many problems connected with loans (29:1-7, 14-20). According to Sirach wealth is not wrong, but he sharply criticizes ill-gotten gains (4:1-3; 5:8; 21:8) and warns that it is difficult for the rich to remain honest and faithful to God (26:29-27:2; 31:1-11).

SIRACH'S AFFIRMATIONS ABOUT THE POOR

What Sirach has to say about the poor in a positive way reflects earlier tradition which equates the poor with the righteous (12:1-5), yet the author does not idealize the state of poverty:

> "My son, do not lead the life of a beggar; it is better to die than to beg. When a man looks to the table of another, his existence cannot be considered as life." (40:28-29)

These verses together with Sirach's admonitions to the wealthy to be charitable to the poor and his condemnation of those who take advantage of the poor indicate that he considered poverty to be an aberration which can and should be eliminated if people would live according to the divine will. He recognizes the basic equality of rich and poor lies in their relationship to God: "The rich, and the eminent, and the poor—their glory is the fear of the Lord" (10:22). He therefore recognizes and praises those poor whose understanding brings them close to God (10:23; 11:1). Finally Sirach suggests that his upper class readers adopt the attitude of the poor since it is the key to experiencing divine mercy (3:17-19). Sirach notes that Moses was chosen by God precisely because he possessed this attitude (45:4)

CONCLUSION

There is certainly some tension in the words of Sirach. On the one hand, he recognizes the socio-economic problems of his own society and criticizes them with the intensity of a prophet. On the other hand, however, he reflects the wisdom tradition's approach to the problems of life which can sometimes appear to be somewhat self-centered. He praises those who have gained their wealth honestly and he criticizes those who have become poor because of their own failings. He finds the life of those reduced to begging as worse than death. Much stronger, however, are Sirach's warnings against the problems that come with wealth and his call for generosity toward the poor. Sirach condemns the power of the rich who often make unscrupulous use of that power to the detriment of the poor. Sirach is speaking to those Jews who were enjoying prosperity as a result of their collaboration with their Greek masters. Throughout his book, Sirach warns his readers about the dark side to this collaboration. When speaking about the poor, Sirach reflects not only his wisdom background but also the prophetic criticism of a social situation in which the poor were oppressed by the wealthy. Sirach does not idealize poverty but warns about the kinds of attitudes and actions by the rich that breed and perpetuate poverty against the divine will.

The Wisdom of Solomon

The Book of Wisdom, which is also known as the Wisdom of Solomon, has a quite different purpose from that of Sirach. The Book of Wisdom attempts to show how Hellenistic perspectives can be combined with the traditions of Yahwism. The book was probably written in Alexandria, a thoroughly Hellenistic city with a very large Jewish population. In that milieu, Jews certainly could not afford to be completely isolated from their cultural environment. This book is a good example of how early Judaism outside of

Palestine was able to express traditional beliefs in another cultural framework. The book itself was written in Greek rather than Hebrew.

The contents of the Wisdom of Solomon are tradition when it comes to the question of how the poor are to be treated. Indeed the book begins with an exhortation to justice as the way to immortality (1:1-15). This is followed by a speech given by the wicked whose way leads to death (1:16-2:24). The speech describes how the wicked plot against the "poor honest man" (2:10-20). The wicked do not hesitate to go so far as to condemn the poor to death. Because the poor remain faithful, they will be granted immortality and will be in a position "to judge nations" (3:6-9).

As is the case with the biblical tradition in general, the Book of Wisdom also sees God as the vindicator of the poor who are oppressed. The principal difference in the approach taken in the Wisdom of Solomon is that this divine vindication is something which takes place after death. The death of the poor merely looks as if it were their final defeat, but the gift of immortality which is given to the just enables the poor to survive the persecution of the unjust and arise in judgment over their former tormentors.

The Book of Tobit

The story of Tobit, an example of Jewish folklore from the beginning of the 2nd century B.C., underscores the importance of kindness towards the poor. The story is about a good man who was stricken with blindness. Because this handicap prevented Tobit from working, poverty was the inevitable result yet he advises his son not to be concerned:

> "Do not be afraid, my son, because we have become poor. You have great wealth if you fear God and refrain from every sin and do what is pleasing in his sight" (Tob 4:21).

Even though his wife questions the value of almsgiving (2:14), Tobit still finds value in it. Both the rich and the poor should give alms: "If you have many possessions, make your gift from them in proportion; if few, do not be afraid to give according to the little you have" (4:8). Tobit is convinced that by being generous to the poor, he would be prepared for the day when fortunes will be reversed. Indeed at the end of the story, Tobit's sight is restored and the book praises him as an almsgiver both before and after his affliction (Tob 1:3 and 14:2). In the Book of Tobit the poor are presented favorably as those to whom charity is due. God rewards almsgiving with forgiveness of sin and the fullness of life (12:9). There is no hint of a denigration of the poor as responsible for their own plight. Though Tobit and his family become poor, the book does not idealize poverty. In fact, the book shows how Tobit's fidelity and charity are rewarded and his poverty overcome.

The Testaments of the Twelve Patriarchs

Benevolence towards the poor is a topic that emerges with the Testaments of the Twelve Patriarchs.[8] These texts which date from the second century B.C. are presented as the last words of Jacob's sons to their children. They contain the kind of practical advice and ethical values which are characteristic of wisdom literature. Issachar advises his sons to value hard work (TIss 5:3-5). This text implies that the quality of one's work has something to do with one's economic prosperity. This is basically consistent with the perspective of Proverbs. The Testaments also value benevolence toward the poor and the weak: "Love the Lord and your neighbor, be compassionate toward poverty and sickness' (TIss 5:2). The Testaments also excoriate those who

[8]For an introduction to and the text of the Testaments of the Twelve Patriarchs see H.C. Kee, "Testaments of the Twelve Patriarchs," in *The Old Testament Pseudepigrapha*. James H. Charlesworth, ed. (Garden City: Doubleday, 1983), v. 1, pp. 775-828.

are guilty of oppression and injustice but mask these by charity toward the poor: "Someone steals, deals unjustly, robs, cheats, but yet has pity on the poor. This...has two aspects but is evil as a whole" (TAsh 2:5). Thus charity and justice were both concerns in the Testaments. Occasionally passages from the Testaments betray an apocalyptic perspective regarding the poor: "...And they who were poor for the Lord's sake shall be made rich..." (TJud 25:4). The text assures the reader that poverty will be abolished in the world to come. Again there is no hint of any idealization of the poor. They are presented as objects of charity.

Conclusion

Except for the psalms, most of the statements made in the Bible about the poor are found in the wisdom literature of ancient Israel and early Judaism. Its views of poverty are quite realistic, for this literature recognizes that poverty may at times be one's own fault—an idea not found in the prophets or the psalms. At the same time, this tradition recognizes the responsibility of the rich for creating and perpetuating poverty. It criticizes the rich on this score and calls for understanding of and charity toward the poor. The approach towards the poor in the wisdom tradition can best be characterized as neutral in the sense that the origins of poverty are traced to laziness and folly as well as oppression and injustice. What the tradition is not neutral about is the responsibility of people of means towards the poor. Poverty calls for action from the wealthy to alleviate the burdens of those poor.

Select Bibliography

Bergant, Dianne, C.S.A., *Job, Ecclesiastes.* Old Testament Message, 18. Wilmington: Michael Glazier, 1982.

Brueggemann, Walter, *In Man We Trust.* Atlanta: Knox, 1972.

Cox, Dermot, O.F.M., *Proverbs.* Old Testament Message, 17. Wilmington: Michael Glazier, 1982.

Crenshaw, James L., *Old Testament Wisdom.* Atlanta: Knox, 1981.

Murphy, Roland E., O. Carm., *Wisdom Literature & Psalms.* Interpreting Biblical Texts. Nashville: Abingdon, 1983.

6

The Poor in the Psalms

Introduction

The Psalter is replete with references to the poor. Here the poor are idealized. Here poverty takes on an aura of sanctity as if it possessed a religious character. In the psalms, the poor are meek, lowly, humble, faithful, righteous, dependent, hopeful. The poor have surrendered themselves completely to God. This is especially evident in psalms of lament (e.g. Pss 3, 5, 6, 44, 74, 79, 83). The form which these psalms follow reflects a liturgical pattern. An invocation of God is followed by the psalmist's petitions for deliverance. The psalm concludes with an expression of trust in God. The psalmist turns to God because God is the protector and refuge of the poor. God combats those who would prevent the poor from securing their rights. Others may fall, but God will always be help to the poor in need.

In the psalms the poor individual is contrasted with those who are unrighteous. The poor person has the quality of authenticity. Since the rich are the oppressors, the poor person is always presented as the "righteous one." In the psalms, the poor become the pious. The traditional ancient

Near Eastern concept of God as the protector of the poor takes on an added dimension here since the poor are equated with the righteous and therefore are most deserving of divine protection. In his commentary on the psalms, Artur Weiser maintains that the designation of those who are faithful to Yahweh as "needy" and "poor" originates in the cult itself rather than in any existential situation. Literally the words translated as "poor" and "needy" in the psalms (*'ani, 'anaw*) mean "bent low" and refer to the outward and inward posture of those who stand before Yahweh in submission and adoration. He considers the use of these words to describe social distinctions between the people and their oppressive rulers as secondary.[1]

In reading the psalms, A. Gelin like Weiser is convinced that these prayers, when referring to the poor, did not refer to "mere sociological status" but to those who were obedient to the Lord.[2] He goes on to describe what he considers to be a spirituality of the poor. Poverty no longer refers to a socio-economic situation but to an inner attitude, a moral ideal, a spiritual value. One question this chapter will have to deal with is the legitimacy of such a reading of the psalms.

The psalms are, after all, prayers; therefore, a certain amount of "spiritualization" is to be expected. The question needs to be focused on the portrait of the poor presented in these prayers. Are the poor of the psalms the materially poor? How do the psalms evaluate poverty? What is the purpose of the prayer which calls God to defend and save the poor? Do these prayers seem to call for a kind of voluntary poverty? These are some of the questions which a reading of the psalms poses for those who wish to understand their view of the poor.

---

[1] Artur Weiser, *The Psalms.* Old Testament Library. (Philadelphia: Westminster, 1962), p. 93.

[2] Gelin, *The Poor of Yahweh,* pp. 36-37.

Social Conflict in the Psalms

The Psalms of Lament make it clear that the situation in which the poor find themselves is caused by "enemies" (9:4-7; 35:19; 65:5, 19). While sometimes rather vague terms are used to describe these enemies such as "the wicked" (10:4; 12:9; 140:5, 9), other times rather specific terms are used that make it clear that these enemies are the wealthy who take advantage of the poor: "despoilers" (35:10), "plunderers" (109:11), "creditors" (109:11), and perjured witnesses (35:11; 109:31). While these psalms use a variety of terms to describe the "enemies" of the poor, clearly some of these terms reflect a situation of socio-eonomic conflict within the Israelite community. This conflict is described as one involving the very survival of the poor:

> "The wicked draw the sword and bend their bows, to bring down the poor and the needy, to slay those who walk uprightly...." (37:14 see also 109:16)

At least in some of the psalms, the poor are those who are the losers in the conflict—they are the materially poor.

There is one suggestion that a number of psalms reflect the prayers of the oppressed to seek refuge from their creditors within the Temple.[3] The Temple would serve as a place of asylum. In accordance with this suggestion Psalm 86 is a prayer expecting an oracle of protection against overzealous creditors:

> "Incline thy ear, O Lord, and answer me, for I am poor and needy...O God, insolent men have risen up against me...and save the son of your handmaid...Show me a sign of thy favor." (vv. 1, 14, 16, 17)

According to this suggestion words like "refuge," "stronghold," and "protection," which are often used in the psalms

---

[3]L. Delekat, *Asylie und Schutzorakel am Zionheiligtum.* (Leiden: Brill, 1967).

of lament originally referred to sanctuaries where the poor found relief from the hounding of their creditors. It was only later that these words became spiritualized to mean communion with God. It is clear that the poor did find in the Temple a place where they prayed for legal aid and righteous judgment (10:12-18; 35:22-24; 140:12). The language here is not all metaphorical. It reflects the social conflict within ancient Israel that is evident when reading the Former and Latter Prophets. This prophetic material reports and condemns the oppression of the poor. The psalms give an insight into how the poor handled the conflict. They had none of the power possessed by the wealthy. All they had was prayer.

The poor were, however, to have more than just a prayer for justice. The king was to be God's instrument for securing justice on behalf of the poor and oppressed. Psalm 72 is a prayer for divine blessing on the king. It asks that God's justice be given to the king so that the king may, in turn, judge the people in righteousness which means nothing less than the poor receiving their due (vv. 1-2). The psalm asserts that it is the king who was to defend the poor and deal with their oppressors (v. 4). If the king is faithful to this responsibility, he will be rewarded with universal dominion (vv. 8-14). This text certainly reflects social conflict within Israel. Here again the "poor" are the economically marginal who are in danger of exploitation and who are to be protected by the king.

The king is the protector of the poor because he stands in God's place. The role of the gods as protectors of the poor is a commonplace in ancient Near Eastern theology. Psalm 82 makes use of another common ancient Near Eastern belief— that the world is ruled by a council of gods. The psalmist sees a vision of that council in which the God of Israel rebukes the members of the divine council for governing the world unjustly (v. 2). The sentence God pronounces on the members of the council for their failure is death. God fully expects that the powerless in society be accorded justice and that the weak be delivered from their oppressors (vv. 3-5).

Again there is no hint of idealizing the state of the poor. Injustice and oppression are contrary to God's will for this world. Those who countenance these can expect divine judgment.

If there is a spiritualization of the poor in these psalms, it is the result of a secondary development. Psalms 72, 82, 86 and a number of individual psalms of lament are talking about real oppression of the economically poor. Rather than idealizing the situation of the poor as a state of special closeness to God these psalms envision relief for the poor through the institutions of society. One effect of God's choice of the Davidic dynasty and Jerusalem is the alleviation of the hunger of the poor:

> "I will abundantly bless her provisions; I will satisfy her poor with bread." (132:15)

God as Protector of the Poor

While the psalms do give some indication of some societal structures which were to protect the poor, these prayers focus their attention on Yahweh who is praised as the protector and deliverer of the poor (9:12, 18; 10:14; 35:2; 68:11; 69:34; 107:41; 109:31; 113:7; 140:12; 147:6; 149:4). The worshipper who experiences oppression asks for protection and strength (12:1; 69:35). The poor are the clients of God (Pss 10, 25, 34, 37, 82). The poor offer this prayer for God's help because of their faith in the goodness, love and fidelity of God (69:13-15; 86:5, 15). One image of the divine that comes to the fore in these prayers is that of God as Judge (Ps 9). The poor pray that God will vindicate them according to divine righteousness (35:23-24), maintain their cause and execute justice (140:12). Sometimes God's protection of the poor comes indirectly. Psalm 41:1 pronounces a blessing on those who remember the plight of the poor and Psalm 112:5, 9 praises people who lend with justice and distribute their goods to the poor.

Those that are not poor in a material sense, of course, desire the same sort of divine protection; consequently, the terms for "poor" in the psalms are extended in their meaning beyond their original denotation and come to include all those who seek God's help (109:22). Similarly, the deliverance these people seek is not limited to the reversal of socio-economic oppression but comes to include almost every need. The poor then become all those who have not experienced the divinely willed fullness of life. But it remains true that the original focus of these prayers was on the alleviation of socio-economic oppression that resulted from the social conflict in ancient Israel which is described in the prophetic corpus.

The 'anawim

Most often words for "the poor" in the psalms are singular except in some of the later psalms when the plural form *'anawim* begins to appear (Ps 9:19; 10:16; 22:26; 34:2; 37:11; 69:32; 76:9; 147:6; 149:4). It appears as if this word is an "established form" adopted from real life.[4] Here is where Gelin focuses his attention—on a "movement" of *'anawim* or humble pious.[5] He sees the members of this group forming the religious nucleus of the nation in contrast to their opponents who are ready to abandon their ancestral religion.[6] What is clear from the reading of the psalms in which the word *'anawim* appears is that allusions to material poverty or the problems of the poor are missing. Here the primary social conflict is no longer simply on an economic level but appears to be on the religious level. While poverty still

[4]E. Bammel, *"ptochos, ptochei, ptocheuo,"* Theological Dictionary of the New Testament. [*TDNT*], vol. 6, p. 892.

[5]There is not universal acceptance of the existence of such a movement. See Bammel, p. 893 note 61; Leander E. Keck, "Poor," *Interpreter's Dictionary of the Bible.* Supplementary volume, p. 673.

[6]See Gelin, *The Poor of Yahweh,* pp. 38-42.

existed, the conflict with the wealthy was seen to be determined not by their economic practices but by their approach to their ancestral religion. In the eyes of the *'anawim,* the wealthy were not true believers—they were evil. Conservative Jews, no matter what their economic status, considered themselves to be among the poor. The words for "poor" become functionally equivalent to "pious" or "humble" and the opposite of "evil" and "wicked."

Even though one may speak of a type of "spiritualization" of poverty and the poor in the Book of Psalms, these prayers nevertheless do not detach themselves completely from earlier perspectives on the poor and they do not idealize the state of poverty as such. The intensity of the language in the psalms of lament make it clear that the "poor" did not accept their situation as the divine will. They beg for deliverance. They ask for the defeat of their enemies. They pray for vindication. By no means are they resigned to the situation which they experience as oppressive. Secondly, those who pray these psalms fully expect that they will be vindicated by God. Submission does not mean the quiet acceptance of oppression. It refers to the confidence that the expected deliverance will take place in accord with the divine good pleasure. The "humility" of the *'anawim* consisted in the acknowledgement that only God was able to save them. Indeed the *'anawim* understand and accept God's justice, providence and will in their totality because they understand that God's will is for the vindication of the just. The reason why the conservatives reinterpreted the cries of the poor in their own conflicts with those whom they considered to be the "wicked" was precisely because the poor fully expected justice from God.[7]

---

[7]It is doubtful that the appropriation of the term *'anawim* indicated any attempt at achieving solidarity with the material poor through voluntary poverty. Like the material poor the *'anawim* experienced themselves as marginated in their society and thus appropriating the language of poverty and the poor was natural.

Psalms 9 and 10[8]

A. Gelin agrees with the opinion that Psalms 9 and 10 reflect the ideology of the *'anawim* most clearly.[9] What do these psalms say about the attitude of the *'anawim?* The ones who pray this psalm include themselves among those who trust in God (9:10). They also call themselves "poor" [*'ani*] (10:2, 9) and "humble" [*'anawim*] (10:17). Because they are oppressed by ungodly adversaries, they see themselves as in the same situation as the poor and afflicted (9:9, 12, 18; 10:8-10, 12, 14). They pray this psalm of lament in which they describe the evil of their oppressors in great detail in order to be delivered from their enemies (10:1-15). This lament is placed within a context which celebrates Yahweh who is enthroned as king in order to judge the nations (9:4, 7-8, 19; 10:16). None of this suggests a humble acceptance of oppression and poverty as the divine will. None of this idealizes poverty as a state of special closeness to God. Those who prayed this psalm regarded their situation as "abnormal." That is precisely why they pray for the righteous judgment of God. Those who pray this psalm are confident of being heard because they are convinced of the righteousness of their cause as compared to that of their oppressors and the power of God to move against those who are responsible for oppression. The use of vocabulary associated with the poor reflects an attempt to identify with the poor in their oppression and thereby guarantee deliverance. The psalm ends with a confident statement that God will indeed bring an end to the oppression of the "poor" (19:17-18). There is no hint whatever in this psalm of any

---

[8]In their original form Psalms 9 and 10 probably made up a single psalm. In the Septuagint these two psalms appear as one psalm. Additional support is the similarity and sometimes identity of expression in both psalms, the lack of a title for Psalm 10 and the traces of an acrostic scheme that embraces both the psalms. An acrostic psalm is one in which the initial words of each verse were arranged according to a particular pattern. Other examples are Psalms 25, 34, 37, 111, 112, 119, and 145.

[9]Gelin, *The Poor of Yahweh,* p. 54.

type of religious acceptance of oppression. What the poor accept is their dependence upon God—not their oppression.

The Prayers for an End of Oppression

Another example of this same kind of identification with the poor is found in Psalm 12. This psalm is a personal lament. In the course of the lament comes the assurance of being heard. Here that assurance is given in v.5 where God asserts that action will be taken on behalf of the poor and needy:

> "Because the poor are despoiled, because the needy groan, I will now arise, says the Lord; I will place them in the safety for which they long."

Again there is no hint of humble acceptance of oppression. In fact, the assurance made to the suppliant is based on the belief that God will not allow the suffering of the poor to go on indefinitely. Psalm 14:6 is also based on the assurance that God will act on behalf of the poor and frustrate the plans of their oppressors. In fact, many of the references made to the poor assume that God will bring an end to their oppression (e.g. 18:27; 22:26; 34:7; 35:10; 40:17; 69:34; 70:5; 74:19, 21; 76:9; 86:1). There is not a single instance in the psalms when the poor or those who identify with them appear to accept their oppression as the divine will. In fact, Psalm 37:11 promises that the *'anawim* will "possess the land."[10]

Indeed there would be more of a problem if the psalmists expressed a kind of resignation to the experience of oppression. Israel's encounter with God which is celebrated in the cult is remembered as an experience of Israel's need and God's response. In Egypt Israel complains of its

---

[10] Jesus apparently had this text in mind in the Sermon on the Mount (Matt 5:5). The Semitic word behind the word translated as "meek" is probably *'anawim*.

oppression under Pharaoh and God frees the people from that oppression. In the wilderness, the people complain of thirst and hunger and God provides water from the rock and manna from heaven. At the time of the conquest, the people complain that Canaan is inhabited by people who cannot be dislodged and God grants Israel victory. When these stories are told, the distress of the Israelites is graphically described, their cry of distress directed to Yahweh is recounted, God's promise of deliverance is recalled, the actual deliverance is celebrated and the people respond in praise of God.[11] Israel experienced and celebrated God as one who saves from oppression—not one requiring humble submission to oppression. Notice that part of the process of deliverance is the cry for help. Thus the prayers we find in the psalms are to be understood not so much as idealizations of poverty but as a component of the process that will eventually lead to an end of oppression. It appears as if such cries to God for help are a significant part of the interchange that goes on between God and Israel.

In this context, how is it possible for those who lament their own oppression and suffering to go away in submission? The psalms of lament take seriously human sinfulness and failure but they do not believe that God's actions on behalf of the just ought to be limited by human failure. The reason people bring their complaints to God is because they are convinced of receiving a hearing. Were it otherwise the laments of the psalter would be nothing more than an exercise in self-pity. Since the laments are addressed to the one who can remove suffering, they are much more. They are an affirmation that oppression is not something to be endured with patience but is something that is to be brought before God.

The Bible presents material poverty as an evil. Because the paslms have reinterpreted the vocabulary of material poverty to speak about "the ability to welcome God, an openness to

---

[11]This pattern can be recognized in the prayer Deuteronomy suggests be said when first fruits are brought to the Temple (Deut 26:5-11): distress (v. 6), the cry for help (7a), God hears (7b), the deliverance (8-9) and the response (10-11).

God, a willingness to be used by God, a humility before God,"[12] there is the temptation to believe that the poor have been "canonized," as if material poverty gave people special access to God without any choice on the part of the poor themselves—a type of socio-economic path to salvation. A second temptation is to consider the Bible's criticism of those responsible for poverty as somehow muted. There is no justification for ignoring the Bible's critique of the selfishness which causes oppression and which divides humanity into rich and poor, possessors and dispossessed, oppressors and oppressed. It is clear that the psalms of lament call for divine action to end poverty and oppression.

Select Bibliography

Stuhlmueller, Carroll, C.P., *Psalms 1 and 2*. Old Testament Message, 21 and 22. Wilmington: Michael Glazier, 1983.

Weiser, Artur, *The Psalms*. The Old Testament Library. Philadelphia: Westminster, 1962.

[12]Gelin, *The Poor of Yahweh*, p. 33.

7

The Poor in Apocalyptic Literature

Introduction: Definitions

The word apocalyptic can refer to a way of looking at reality, a literary form and a body of literature. It is helpful to define this term in each of these connections. First, as a way of interpreting human experience, apocalyptic has been described as "a Judeo-Christian world-view which located the believer in a minority community and gave his life meaning by relating it to the end, soon to come, which would reverse his present status."[1] The impulse behind such a perspective on human experience is a genuine restlessness and total dissatisfaction with the evils of the present and the desire for a new and total solution to the human problem.

---

[1] William A. Beardslee, "New Testament Apocalyptic in Recent Interpretation," *Interpretation* 25/4 (1971), p. 424. Sometimes apocalyptic as a world-view is called "apocalypticism." Another very helpful profile of the apocalyptic world-view is given by Klaus Koch, *The Rediscovery of Apocalyptic.* (London: SCM, 1972), pp. 28-33.

Apocalyptic can also refer to a literary form: the apocalypse. The latter has been defined as

> "...a genre of revelatory literature with a narrative framework, in which a revelation is mediated by an otherworldly being to a human recipient, disclosing a transcendent reality which is both temporal, insofar as it envisages eschatological salvation, and spatial insofar as it involves another, supernatural world."[2]

Finally the term apocalyptic refers to a body of literature. The only two canonical representatives of apocalyptic are the Book of Daniel in the Hebrew Scriptures and the Book of Revelation in the New Testament. There is a greater number of extra-canonical texts that fall into this category: 1 Enoch, 2 Enoch, 4 Ezra, 2 Apocalypse of Baruch, the Apocalypse of Abraham.[3]

Apocalyptic literature first emerged in the third century B.C. and has had a permanent influence on Judaism and Christianity.[4] An apocalyptic text describes visions experienced by a seer. Since these visions are highly symbolic and mystifying, they are interpreted to the seer usually by an

---

[2]John J. Collins, "Introduction: Towards the Morphology of a Genre," *Semeia* 14 (1979), p. 9.

[3]There is some debate about the inclusion of other ancient texts in this category. See Michael E. Stone, "Apocalyptic Literature," in *Jewish Writings of the Second Temple Period,* M.E. Stone, ed. (Philadelphia: Fortress, 1984), pp. 393-394. See also John J. Collins, "Jewish Apocalypses," *Semeia* 14 (1979), pp. 21-60.

For an introduction to these books see Leonhard Rost, *Judaism Outside the Hebrew Canon.* (Nashville: Abingdon, 1976) and G.E.W.Nickelsburg, *Jewish Literature Between the Bible and the Mishnah.* (Philadelphia: Fortress, 1981).

[4]Even though the rabbis rejected the apocalypses except for Daniel, still their influence has been felt in the development of messianism and mysticism. See J. Block, *On the Apocalyptic in Judaism.* (Philadelphia: Fortress, 1952) and A.J. Saldarini, "Apocalypses and 'Apocalyptic' in Rabbinic Literature and Mysticism," *Semeia* 14 (1979), pp. 187-206.

The influence of apocalyptic in Christianity has been to heighten its eschatological thrust. See Adela Yarbro Collins, "The Early Christian Apocalypses," *Semeia* 14 (1979), pp. 61-122.

angel who explains the meaning and implication of the images in the vision. The account of the vision is not published in the name of its writer but is attributed to a famous figure of the past. Although these books were originally Jewish works and written in the languages understood by Jews in the Second Temple period (Hebrew, Aramaic and Greek), they have been transmitted almost exclusively by Christian communities. Most have survived not in their original languages but in those of the communities which have preserved them.

There are three features of apocalyptic texts that are especially important. The first is the revelation of heavenly secrets which very often have decidedly political overtones. The second is apocalyptic's brand of eschatology which looks for an imminent end to this world. Finally there is the pessimism of apocalyptic texts regarding the possibilities of positive change in this world. The origin of apocalyptic as a way of interpreting experience was grounded on the experience of the collapse of a previously accepted world-view which set forth values and gave a semblance of order to experience. With such a collapse people are thrust into a sea of meaninglessness.

The Origin of Apocalyptic

Apocalyptic emerges in response to this situation. It purports to provide information about the future of this world which could be obtained only from someone who has been privy to the secrets of the heavens. The esoteric knowledge that apocalyptic imparts is really information about the political sphere, about the future God has planned for this world and its powers. The quest for such knowledge became acute when it was perceived that the well-defined structures of the Torah as interpreted by the prophets were not a sufficient guide to those Jews who felt that they were among the marginated in the Second Temple Period. The Law and the Prophets spoke to people who were assumed to be in control of their own destiny, to people who were free to make decisions about the future, to people who were able to shape events. The Jews of the Second Temple period, for the most part, were not these kind of people.

First of all, during this period Judah was not really an independent state except for the period of Hasmonean rule (165-63 B.C.). Without such status, the Jews were not able to make the kind of fundamental political and economic decisions that would have allowed them to control their own destiny. Judah was either completely subject to or at least a client state of the Persian, Hellenistic or Roman Empires for the greater part of the time when apocalyptic flourished. Secondly Paul Hanson has described a rift within the Jewish community itself between the priestly hierocracy and the visionaries who considered themselves to be heirs of the prophetic tradition.[5] The priestly group accepted the status of Judah as a minor province of the Persian Empire. They defined restoration as the reestablishment of the Temple cult as it had existed before the Exile. The visionaries saw the restoration in the glorious terms described by Second Isaiah (Isa 40-55). When the restoration did not take place according to the expectations of their mentor, the disciples of Second Isaiah blamed the corruption of the priestly party (see Isa 58:1-12). Before long there was a great rift between the two groups.[6] The disciples of the prophets saw themselves as locked out of the restoration and increasingly marginated because of the domination of the priestly hierocracy. The visionaries felt oppressed and looked to God for relief: "...Your brethren who hate you and cast you out for my name's sake have said, 'Let the Lord be glorified...'; but it is they who shall be put to shame" (Isa 66:5). At a point when the disciples of Second Isaiah no longer felt the prospects of any real change in their situation they gave up on the possibilities of the present and began to envision salvation

---

[5] *The Origin of Apocalyptic.* (Philadelphia: Fortress, 1975).

[6] See Isaiah 57, 59, 65, 66 to get a feeling of the acrimony and bitterness between these two groups.

on a timeless, cosmic level. They no longer saw the possibility of any change in their own political, religious, economic or social status. They looked for another world in which their unpleasant situation would be reversed. A number of apocalypses seem to reflect a setting of persecution. These apocalypses reveal to the faithful a vision of a new day and a new world in which salvation and glorification will take place (e.g. Dan 12:1). In other words, some people no longer believed that God's promises could be fulfilled in the present order. They looked for a new world—a new age in which divine justice would rule. This way of handling the social and religious conflict within early Judaism was easily adaptable to the conflicts in the realm of external politics. Certain of the apocalypses were violently anti-Seleucid or anti-Roman.[7]

The basic assumption of all apocalypses is that this world is disordered. It is controlled by sinners and by the gentiles. There will come a day when the just will be vindicated by God and be victorious over their enemies. The apocalyptic seer describes his visions in order to assure the just that that day and that new world are coming soon. By postponing the full revelation of divine justice into another age, apocalyptic handles some very difficult theological problems (divine justice, reward and punishment) in a manner that helps explain to people who feel oppressed because justice in this world is not forthcoming. There is simply no justice in this world.

Daniel

The Book of Daniel is a product of the Hellenistic period of Judah's history. The tales (chapters 1-6)[8] were probably

---

[7]Daniel, The Testament of Moses, and portions of 1 Enoch were written during the persecution of Antiochus IV, the Seleucid Emperor who proscribed the practice of Judaism in 167 B.C. while 4 Ezra, 2 Baruch and the Apocalypse of Abraham were written following the Roman destruction of the Temple in A.D 70.

[8]Other tales about Daniel which have become associated with the Book of Daniel are the deuterocanonical chapters 13 and 14. These are not found in the Hebrew

written somewhat earlier than the visions (chapters 7-12) which were composed during the Maccabean revolution (167-164 B.C.)[9] The book was written so that the people could benefit from the teaching of the *maskilim* (the wise) in time of persecution (Dan 11). According to this teaching some of the people would be killed in the course of the persecution but at the time of the resurrection they will shine in the heavens and be like the stars forever (12:1-4). It has been suggested that these *maskilim* were upper-class, well-educated Jews who were civil servants in the Diaspora and who would be predisposed to maintaining the status quo. They were, however, completely loyal to their ancestral religion.[10] The tales about Daniel (chapters 1-6) show how it is possible to straddle the two different worlds of royal service and traditional Judaism.

With this kind of social setting, it is understandable why the poor go unmentioned except for a single instance in the tales of Daniel. The questions of justice, social conflict, exploitation and oppression seemed less important than strategies for maintaining people's loyalty to their ancestral religion. The one time the poor are mentioned (4:24) it is in an admonition to Nabuchadnezzar, the king of Babylon. The king is told that mercy towards the poor may bring peace in his own life.

The setting of the visions (chapters 7-12) is somewhat different. The scene of activity of the *maskilim* has changed from the Diaspora to Jerusalem. Similarly, the attitude of the gentile rulers toward the Jews changed from tolerance

Bible but are found in the Septuagint and Vulgate and so are considered canonical in the Roman Catholic tradition.

[9]John J. Collins, *Daniel, with an Introduction to Apocalyptic Literature.* The Forms of the Old Testament Literature, XX. (Grand Rapids: Eerdmans, 1984), p. 36. Conservative scholars prefer to date the book in the Babylonian Period (6th cen. B.C.) which is the setting given in Daniel, e.g. Desmond Ford, *Daniel.* (Nashville: Southern Publishing Assoc., 1978), pp. 30-44. The evidence for dating Daniel to the Maccabean period, however, is quite convincing.

[10]John J. Collins, "Daniel and His Social World," *Interpretation* 39/2 (1985), pp. 136-137.

and even sympathy to opposition and persecution.[11] The conflict with the king is over religious matters and is not conceived as the result of socio-economic and political problems faced by the king. A reconstruction of the period of Seleucid rule, however, shows a genuine social conflict among the Jewish community, which was divided between the ruling classes which endorsed a thoroughgoing hellenization of Judah and the majority of the largely poor population which opposed this development. At this time the office of high priest was sold to the highest bidder by the Seleucids who used the money to finance their wars. During one of these wars waged by the Seleucids against their rivals, the Ptolemies, traditionalists in Jerusalem revolted against Seleucid rule. The success of this revolution was short-lived and Antiochus reconquered Jerusalem and exacted heavy tribute from the people, and the high priest who was in league with Antiochus even helped strip the Temple of its gold (1 Macc 1:21-28). Two years later Antiochus began a full-scale persecution of the traditionalists among the Jews whom he saw as disloyal and troublesome.[12] There certainly was division within the Jewish community during this period. This division was largely economic with religious overtones. Daniel largely ignores this division and defines the conflict as if it were a purely religious one between the faithful of Judaism and the faithless king. Daniel 11 does shed some light on the social conflict within the Jewish community as it distinguishes three groups among the Jews: those "who forsake the holy covenant" (v. 30), "the people who know their God" (v. 31) and "the many" (v. 34). The fate of the last group mentioned is apparently determined by what side they choose.

[11]While Daniel blames the persecution of the Jews solely on the king, 1 Maccabees also places some of the blame on certain "lawless men" who sought accommodations with the Greeks (1 Macc 1:11-15). There certainly was social conflict within Judaism at this time.

[12]See Peter Schäfer, "The Hellenistic and Maccabaen Periods," in *Israelite and Judean History,* J.H. Hayes and J.M. Miller, ed. The Old Testament Library. (Philadelphia: Westminster, 1977), pp. 576-595.

The Book of Daniel, true to the perspective of apocalyptic, sees the final triumph of those who are faithful as the result of God's action through the archangel Michael (Dan 10-12). It rejects the revolutionary spirit of the Maccabees, for goals of the Book of Daniel are not political or economic since this world is passing away. Though the faithful may lose their lives in the course of the persecution, they will be raised to everlasting life (12:2). The book does not offer any temporal, practical solution to problems of the Jewish community which was undergoing persecution.

The Book of Daniel deals with questions of justice from an apocalyptic perspective—one which looks for the imminent intervention of God to reverse the fortunes of the faithful. It offers no practical advice on overcoming injustice since it sees the future as controlled by God alone. There is no justice in this world. Oppression, persecution, poverty are only passing realities as are the kingdoms of this world. What is so critical is that people remain faithful to God despite the problems they face as they struggle to maintain their fidelity. The book's faith in the power of God to control the future enabled those who accepted its message to defy the forces of oppression. There are no practical suggestions for resisting the powers of evil; therefore, a materialist and positivist analysis of Daniel would regard its approach to the problem of oppression as an illusion. Those who first hear its message, however, experience it as life-giving and liberating. The problem comes when contemporary readers try to make Daniel's approach a universal ethic. Among religious Jews of the day there were striking differences of approach to the persecution of Antiochus.[13] Daniel represents one view. Though the book offers no "practical" advice on overcoming oppression, it obviously regards it as an evil which calls forth divine judgment. The "people who know their God" (11:31) are praised not because they suffer persecution but because

[13]See Leslie J. Hoppe, O.F.M., "Religion and Politics: Paradigms from Early Judaism," in *Biblical and Theological Reflection on* The Challenge of Peace, J.T. Pawlikowski and D. Senior, eds. (Wilmington: Michael Glazier, 1984), pp. 45-54.

they remain faithful to their God despite the suffering that they have to endure. Daniel affirms that this suffering will end by the power of God.

1 Enoch

A better look into the social conflicts going on within the Jewish community is provided by another apocalypse: 1 Enoch. One of its principal features is its condemnation of economic exploiters, political oppressors and all those guilty of unjust social conduct. The value of this work is that it shows the depth of resentment that existed among the poor towards the Jewish aristocracy.

Chapters 92-105 of 1 Enoch is a letter written in the name of Enoch.[14] Though the letter is addressed to Enoch's children, its message is intended for those people of the writer's own day. The purpose of this letter is to provide the assurance God is coming to vindicate the just and punish their oppressors so that with this assurance people can remain faithful in troubled times. The central part of the letter is a series of woes directed at the wicked. The contents of these woes give a fairly clear idea of the world in which the author lives. Some of the crimes for which the wicked are indicted are religious: idolatry (99:7), blasphemy (94:9, 96:7), false teaching (98:15) and the perversion of the Torah (99:2). The bulk of the charges made against the sinners, however, are social and economic:

---

[14]Enoch was one of the antediluvian patriarchs. According to Genesis 5:24 God "took" him. This was interpreted to mean that God removed Enoch from this earth in order to give him a revelation about the end of the age. Enoch wrote this revelation down so that the just living in the last days would have some guidance.

The Book of Enoch is actually a composite work written by different authors over a period of time that may date from the early pre-Maccabean period to just before the Christian era. An introduction and new translation by E. Isaac can be found in *The Old Testament Pseudepigrapha,* J.H. Charlesworth, ed. (Garden City: Doubleday, 1983), pp. 5-89. It is from this translation that all quotations are made in what follows.

"Woe unto you, O rich people...In the days of your affluence, you committed oppression...." (92:8-9)

"Woe unto you, witnesses of falsehood! And unto those who prepare oppression!" (95:6).

"Woe unto you who eat the best bread! And drink wine in large bowls, trampling upon the weak people with your might." (96:5)

"Woe unto you, O powerful people! You who coerce the righteous with your power, the day of your destruction is coming!" (96:8)

"Woe to you who gain silver and gold by unjust means...." (97:8)

"Woe unto you who build your houses through the hard toil of others and your building materials are bricks and stones of sin...." (99:13)

"Woe unto you, sinners, when you oppress the righteous one...." (100:7).

The actions condemned in these woes involve the oppression of the poor. One of the principal theological problems in 1 Enoch is that the experience of the pious does not correspond to their beliefs regarding the way God deals with the just and sinners, with the oppressed and their oppressor. The righteous are not receiving the rewards that should come to them because of their righteousness. In fact, they are experiencing the curses of Deuteronomy 28 which should be inflicted upon sinners (103:9-15). What makes matters even worse is that the righteous are receiving these curses at the hands of sinners. Justice is turned inside out. Sinners flaunt the will of God yet their rebellion goes unpunished. The righteous are not rewarded for their goodness but are oppressed by the wicked.

It is interesting to compare the woes found in Sirach (2:12-14; 41:8-9) with those in 1 Enoch 92-105. Both texts reflect a similar tension between the rich and the poor. Sirach, however, appears to be addressing himself to the rich. He advises them to be concerned about the poor and to use their wealth responsibly to respond to the cries of the needy. Enoch appears to be addressing himself to the poor. He does not foresee any way that the rich can reform themselves. Enoch simply curses them. To the poor he promises an imminent reversal of fortunes in which the injustice and oppression of the present will be eliminated. He consoles the poor by revealing to them that already in the present angels are interceding for them with God, that their names are inscribed in the register of the righteous in heaven and that their salvation is guaranteed (102:4-104:8).

Because 1 Enoch is an apocalypse, it does not foresee the possibility that the situation in this world will change for the poor and oppressed. What the author offers them is the assurance of their eventual deliverance by God. This assurance is to keep them faithful and even joyous in their present suffering. There is not a hint here of an idealization of the poor. They are righteous not because they are poor but because they are faithful to the Law. The wicked are not condemned simply because they are wealthy; they are condemned because of their oppression of the poor.

Qumran

With the discovery of the Dead Sea Scrolls in 1947 and the excavation of the settlement used by those who produced these texts, there are available the physical setting, the literature and some idea of the history of a group of Jews who were imbued with apocalyptic perspectives.[15] The existence of the community in the Judean wilderness and the analysis of the texts which this community valued, produced

[15]Excellent comprehensive treatments of the Dead Sea Scrolls and the community that produced them can be found in Frank M. Cross, *The Ancient Library of Qumran and Modern Biblical Studies.* Revised edition. (Grand Rapids: Baker House, 1961) and Geza Vermes, *The Dead Sea Scrolls.* Revised edition. (Philadelphia: Fortress, 1977).

and transmitted give an insight into the internal debates and social conflicts within Judaism that texts like 1 Enoch witness to.[16] It is clear that these conflicts gave rise to a number of diverse sects and parties so that looking at early Judaism as a monochromatic phenomenon would be a very serious mistake. There is some debate regarding the origins of the community; however, it is clear that the people of Qumran considered themselves to be the only true Israelites.[17] The content and tone of portions of the literature produced by the community itself allows the inference of serious social conflicts within the Jewish community. Of course, these conflicts are presented in religious terms for the most part. They were serious enough for members of the community to leave the population centers of Palestine and establish a settlement for themselves in the uninviting Judean desert near the Dead Sea.

Among the texts produced by the people of Qumran are prayers which are modeled on the psalms of the Bible. These are the *Hodayot* (hymns; 1QH). These are prayers of thanksgiving which praise God for the knowledge and salvation granted to the sect. The use of the term "poor" in these prayers is quite similar to the usage in the biblical psalms. The author of these prayers of thanksgiving identifies himself as a "poor one" whom God has rescued from the opponents of the sect:

> "I thank Thee, O Lord for Thou has [fastened] Thine eye upon me. Thou hast saved me from the zeal of lying interpreters. . .

[16]The Qumran texts which have been found fall into three categories. First are the biblical texts. Texts from every book of the Hebrew Bible except the Book of Esther have been found at Qumran. Secondly the people of Qumran left behind copies of some of the apocrypha and pseudepigrapha of the Old Testament. Though these books were not included in the canon established by the rabbis, evidently they were revered at Qumran. Finally a good portion of the Qumran material includes documents which were produced by and for the community itself.

[17]For a discussion of the history of the community which focuses on the origins of the sect see Devorah Dimant, "Qumran Sectarian Literature," in *Jewish Writings of the Second Temple Period*, pp. 542-547.

Thou hast redeemed the soul of the poor one whom they planned to destroy...."
(1QH 2:31-33; see also 1QH 5:1; 13-14, 15, 18)[18]

In another hymn a larger group are called *'anawim* (poor, meek, humble):

"I thank Thee O Lord, for Thou hast not abandoned the fatherless or despised the poor...wonderful Heroes minister to Thee; yet [hast Thou done marvels] among the humble in the mire underfoot, and among those eager for righteousness, causing all the well-loved poor to rise up together from the trampling." (1QH 5:20-22; *DSSE*, p. 166)[19]

"Thou didst open [his fountain]...[that he might be], according to Thy truth, a messenger [in the season] of thy goodness; that to the humble he might bring glad tidings of thy great mercy...." (1QH 18:14-16; *DSSE*, pp. 199-200)

This has led some interpreters to conclude that "the poor" is a technical term in these hymns and refers to a specific group.[20] In fact, it has been suggested that the Qumran

[18]Two good English translations of some of the Qumran material are Geza Vermes, *The Dead Sea Scrolls in English*. (Baltimore: Penguin, 1962) and Theodor H. Gaster, *The Dead Sea Scriptures*. (Garden City: Doubleday, 1964). Here quotations will be made from the Vermes translation [*DSSE*]. This text can be found on p. 156.

The system for citing Qumran texts is as follows. The first number in the citation indicates the number of the cave in which the particular document was found. The "Q" indicates that the text cited is from Qumran. The next letter or letters is a standard abbreviation for the particular name of the document cited. A list of the standard abbreviations is found on p. xxvi of *The Jerome Biblical Commentary*. (Englewood Cliffs: Prentice-Hall, 1968).

[19]The phrase "well-loved poor" probably reflects the belief of the Qumran people that their life-style is a mark of their election. While this life-style in the Judean desert is not marked by destitution, it can be described as poverty when compared to the usual manner of life that people lived in the cities of Judah.

[20]Bammel, *TDNT*, v. 6, p. 897.

people used the term "the poor" as a self-designation though there is serious doubt that this was the case.[21]

One of the rules of the communty known as the Damascus Document (CD) urges the people of Qumran to remain faithful and assures them that God always rewards fidelity. They are told to be scrupulous in the observance of the Law in an "age of wickedness." Among the sins they are to avoid by separating themselves from the wicked is robbery of the poor and victimizing of the widow and orphan (see CD 6:18; *DSSE,* p. 103). In a more positive tone, the members of the community are told that

> "They shall love each man his brother as himself; they shall succour the poor, the needy, and the stranger." (CD 6:21-22; *DSSE,* p. 103)

In the Damascus Document (CD 14:14) the "poor and needy" are listed among the groups who are to be supported by the community. In these texts, it is clear that "the poor" refers to a socio-economic class and is not a technical term for the Qumran community itself.

The War Rule (1QM) is a special rule covering the eschatological war which the people of Qumran believe would usher in the new age. It is not a military text as much as it is a theological reflection on the continuing struggle between good and evil. This struggle can end only when God steps in to fight on the side of the good. Chapter 11 of that rule reflects the Holy War ideology of the Bible in which those who are least likely to win are those who, in fact, do win by the power of God:

> "For Thou wilt deliver into the hands of the poor the enemies from all the lands, to humble the mighty of the peoples by the hand of those bent to the dust... (1QM 11:13; *DSSE,* p. 138)

---

[21]See Leander E. Keck, "The Poor among the Saints in Jewish Christianity." *Zeitschrift für die Neutestamentliche Wissenschaft* 56 (1965) 76-77.

Here "the poor" are those who have no real power to gain a military victory yet who are triumphant because of the power of God (see also 1QM 13:12-14, *DSSE,* p. 141; 1QM 14:17 *DSSE,* p. 142.). In the War Rule the poor are not so much a socio-economic group as much as they are used to represent the weakness and vulnerability of the faithful.

Included among the distinctive texts of the Qumran community is a collection of exegetical writings which comment on individual books of the Bible. In the commentary on the Book of Habakkuk (1QpHab), the first two chapters of the prophetic book are applied to the history of the community itself. When the author of this text comments on Habakkuk 2:17, he wrote: "Interpreted, this saying concerns the Wicked Priest, inasmuch as he shall be paid the reward which he himself tendered to the poor" (12:2, *DSSE,* p. 242). The author uses familiar phraseology to describe the oppression which the community experienced at the hands of their principal opponent, the Wicked Priest. Exploitation of the powerless by the powerful is a familiar enough theme in the Bible for the author of the commentary to describe the persecution of the Qumran community in precisely that fashion. In another exegetical text, the commentary of Psalm 37 (4Q171 also 4QpPs 37), the focus is again on the conflict between the community and the Wicked Priest. In commenting on Psalm 37:10-11, 22, the author uses the term "the congregation of the poor" (2:9; 3:10, *DSSE,* p. 243-245). Psalm 37 refers to the poor and the needy as those who are persecuted by the wicked who are wealthy (Ps 37:14, 16). In using this text from the psalm to illustrate the Qumran community's history, the author naturally speaks of the community as "poor." Again this does not necessarily refer to the socio-economic status of the community as much as it reflects the community's interpretation of its experience of persecution by the priests of Jerusalem.

Finally, the Qumran community followed the practice of renouncing private property. This is clear enough from the community rule sometimes known as the Manual of Discipline (1QS):

> "They shall separate from the congregation of the men of
> falsehood and shall unite, with respect to the Law and
> possession under the authority of the sons of Zadok ...
> Every decision concerning doctrine, property and justice
> shall be determined by them."
>
> (1QS 5:2, *DSSE*, p. 78)

Those who entered the community were required to transfer
their wealth to the common fund (1QS 1:1-3; 6:17-23;
DSSE, pp. 72, 82). There were penalties for lying about
one's property (6:25, *DSSE*, p. 82) and for failing to care for
the community's property with care (7:6, *DSSE*, p. 83).
These texts do not exhibit a negative attitude toward
possessions as such but indicate the attempt of the community to eliminate distinctions between the wealthy and the
poor which is precisely what will happen in the coming age.

The community of Qumran readily identified itself with
the poor because in the biblical tradition they are the objects
of unjust oppression which is precisely what the Qumran
community believed about itself. There is not enough con-
clusive evidence, however, that this community ever referred
to itself as "The Poor," as if the latter were a technical self-
designation. The community's rule made it clear that
members of the community were not to take advantage of
the poor as the Wicked Priest did. In addition, they were to
contribute to the welfare of the poor with a portion of their
income. Finally, the community attempted to develop a life-
style that did not differentiate between the rich and poor
among its membership because of its belief that no such
distinction would be characteristic of the coming age.

The Psalms of Solomon

While the Dead Sea Scrolls come from a community that
lived in the Judean desert, the Psalms of Solomon come
from Jerusalem in the years just before the coming of

Christ.[22] The perspectives of the Psalms of Solomon and the Dead Sea Scrolls, however, are quite similar. Both are didactic, polemic and theological with a distinct apocalyptic perspective. Though these eighteen poems are called psalms, it is highly unlikely that they would have been used for liturgical purposes. They are basically a poetic treatment of the events in Jerusalem following the Roman conquest in 63 B.C. A prominent feature of this work is its interest in the poor and its criticism of those who have created the social and economic evils in the period when it was written. These psalms convey the author's estimation of the extent to which the Hasmonean dynasty (the descendants of the Maccabees who ruled as kings and high priests in Jerusalem), the government and the cult had become corrupted by the desire for wealth and position.

As is usual in the biblical tradition, God is presented as the protector of the poor (PsSol 5:2, 11; 10:6; 15:1; 18:2). The deplorable situation of the poor is caused by those who were not observant, who were not pious, who were not concerned about the Law. While the economic situation of the poor is not ignored by the psalmist, the focus seems to be on the moral qualities which separate the rich and the poor. The psalmist speaks of the poor and the pious in the same breath:

> "And the devout shall give thanks in the assembly of the people, and God will be merciful to the poor to the joy of Israel." (PsSol 10:6)

The psalmist looked forward to the time when the present situation of oppression will be reversed (PsSol 17:21-34).

Though it may appear as if "the poor" have become spiritualized in the Psalms of Solomon, it is because the author chooses to speak not about their material poverty but

---

[22]For an introduction to and the text of the Psalms of Solomon see R.B. Wright, "Psalms of Solomon" in *The Old Testament Pseudepigrapha,* J.H. Charlesworth, ed., v. 2, pp. 639-670.

about their fidelity to their ancestral religion in comparison with the infidelity of the wealthy that is made so clear through the oppression and corruption that they are responsible for. The psalmist fully expects that there will come a time very shortly when the situation of the poor and the wealthy will be reversed.

The Sibylline Oracles

While the Psalms of Solomon were written in a relatively short period of time just before the Christian Era, the Sibylline oracles were composed over a very long period of time (150 B.C. to A.D. 600).[23] The Sibyl was depicted in antiquity as an old woman who uttered prophecies. She becomes a vehicle of Jewish and Christian prophecy in these oracles. In the Third Book of the oracles, written sometime between 163-45 B.C., the Jews are praised for their social ideals (Sib III:234-247) in comparison with other nations where injustice reigns. The vision that this Third Book has of the future is an idealistic one in which justice will triumph, where there will be material prosperity and above all an end to the exploitation of the poor: "Bad government, blame, envy, anger, folly, poverty will flee from men, and constraint will flee. . .(Sib III:376). The focus in these oracles is not on the socio-economic exploitation taking place within the Jewish community but that which that community experiences because of its subjection to Rome. Though the focus of attention is a different one, this work also looks forward to the day when justice will be established for the poor.

---

[23]For an introduction to and the text of the Sibylline oracles see John J. Collins, "Sibylline Oracles," in *The Old Testament Pseudepigrapha,* J.H. Charlesworth, ed., v. 1, pp. 317-472.

Conclusion

Apocalyptic literature reflects a continuing social and economic conflict between the poor and the wealthy within the Jewish community as well as the problems the Jewish community faced as a result of its lack of political independence. It may very well have been that apocalyptic emerged as a way for the dispossessed within the Jewish community to deal with their experience of oppression. Apocalyptic literature exhibited a point of continuity with earlier biblical tradition when it presented God as the defender of the oppressed. What made apocalyptic unique was its belief that God's intervention on behalf of the oppressed was imminent and that this intervention will usher in a new world. In that new world God's justice will reign and therefore the pious will experience a reversal of fortunes and thereby finally receive the reward for their fidelity in the midst of oppression.

In Daniel this conflict is with gentile rulers who try to proscribe the observance of the Law. The book assures its readers that the power of these rulers is going to come to an end very soon and the faithful will be rewarded with everlasting life. 1 Enoch condemns those within the Jewish community who oppress the poor. The people of the Qumran community look forward to a world in which distinctions between rich and poor will no longer exist. Similarly the Psalms of Solomon and the Sibylline Oracles await the day when the poor will be vindicated and justice will triumph.

At times apocalyptic texts use "the poor" as metaphors for the pious but most often these texts speak about genuine oppression which causes all sorts of problems for the righteous including material poverty. The texts promise speedy vindication for those who remain faithful, for God remains the protector of the oppressed. The state of poverty and oppression is not transformed into some sort of an ideal. It remains an unmitigated evil which God will someday soon overcome with a marvelous display of power. Poverty is not a state of special holiness but it is a scandal that will not exist in the world to come. In that new world, there will be no rich or poor, oppressors or oppressed for it will be the triumph of God's justice.

Select Bibliography

Collins, John J., *The Apocalyptic Imagination.* N.Y.: Crossroad, 1984.

——————, *Daniel.*The Forms of the Old Testament Literature, XX. Grand Rapids: Eerdmans, 1984.

McNamara, Martin, M.S.C., *Intertestamental Literature.* Old Testament Message, 23. Wilmington: Michael Glazier, 1983.

Rowland, Christopher, *The Open Heaven.* N.Y.: Crossroad, 1982.

Stone, Michael E., *Jewish Writings of the Second Temple Period.* Philadelphia: Fortress, 1984.

Vermes, Geza, *The Dead Sea Scrolls.* Revised edition. Philadelphia: Fortress, 1981.

8

The Poor in the New Testament

Introduction

The Hebrew Scriptures and the writings from early Judaism exhibit a wide variety of attitudes toward the poor. The existence of the poor is a sign of Israel's infidelity to the covenant. God is the protector of the poor. The wealthy oppress the poor and cause poverty. In the age to come the poor and the rich will have their roles reversed. People ought to be kind to the poor. Poverty is the result of foolish decisions people make. The poor are those who have an attitude of total dependence upon God. In most of the texts that have been considered, the poor in question are the materially poor. Even in the texts where the poor become metaphors of a religious reality, the socio-economic meanings of this term are never excluded. This should be evident because these ancient Israelite and early Jewish texts do not speak about "poverty." These texts always speak about the poor, the oppressed, the exploited, the widow, the orphan— not about poverty as such. This anchor in socio-economic reality is a key to seeing the context in which the Bible does speak about the so-called *'anawim*. There is no idealization of the poor in the Bible. The poor are blessed not because they are poor but because God is their protector. Both the poor and the wealthy are to observe the Law. The latter are condemned not because they are wealthy but because they do not observe the Law and thereby call divine judgment upon themselves. Without a grounding in a socio-economic reality, the poor of the Bible become nothing more than literary symbols of an attitude of dependence upon God and the Bible's concern for the poor becomes detached from the existential situation of economic need and social injustice. The Bible becomes spiritualized into a caricature of its real self so that it is no longer concerned about material poverty but about something "more important"—spiritual poverty. This is not the tradition of which Jesus of Nazareth is confessed by the Church to be heir and re-interpreter.

This confession is made in the writings of the New Testament. These texts exhibit strong lines of continuity not only with ancient Israelite and early Jewish traditions but are sensitive to the Greco-Roman cultural environment in which those who first heard and read these texts lived. Sometimes the Greco-Roman world is presented as completely devoid of concern for poor.[1] It is perhaps more accurate to say that such concern was rather narrowly defined as limited by an attitude of exclusivism. Concern for the needs of others was expressed by care for one's relatives, friends, fellow citizens and allies rather than by a liberality toward all who may be in need.[2] The Stoics, who believed that humanity was one, taught that benevolence was to be extended to all people. They also taught that wealth was to be shared and poverty endured. A question that still needs to be answered is the extent of the Stoics' influence in the Hellenistic world. Even so, benevolence in the Greco-Roman world was not aimed at eliminating the causes of poverty but

[1]See F. Hauck, *"ptochos,"* *Theological Dictionary of the New Testament*, v. 6, pp. 886-887.

[2]See Glanville Downey, "Who's My Neighbor? The Greek and Roman Answer," *Anglican Theological Review* (1965), pp. 3-15.

simply at relieving its symptoms and therefore it was really not very effective.[3] The New Testament appears in that world and tries to demonstrate the value of the biblical attitude towards the poor.

The Gospels

While the Gospels make some significant statements about the poor, it is important to be certain of the perspective from which these statements are made. It is necessary that interpreters know whether sayings such as "Blessed are you poor" (Lk 6:20) and "What does it profit people to gain the whole world and forfeit their lives?" (Mk 8:36) were made by someone who was rich or poor. Are those statements made as a subtle attempt to preserve privileges of the rich or are they authentic attempts to encourage the poor? Are they calls to justice or are they content to leave the poor in their oppression while conferring on them a certain aura of holiness? The very same saying can have vastly different connotations depending upon the one who is responsible for it.

The gospels portray Jesus of Nazareth as a poor man. There was no place for him to be born (Lk 2:7).[4] Jesus, however, belonged to a family that was not poor. His legal

---

[3]A more comprehensive presentation of the Greco-Roman attitude toward the poor can be found in the unpublished dissertation of Thomas Hoyt, *The Poor in Luke-Acts*. Ph.D. Dissertation, Duke University, 1979.

[4]Raymond Brown sees Luke 2:7 as an allusion to Jeremiah 14:18 which talks about God as an "alien and stranger in the land . . . a traveler who stays in lodgings." According to Brown, the birth of Jesus means that Israel's savior no longer stays in lodgings. See his *The Birth of the Messiah*. (Garden City: Doubleday, 1977), pp. 399-401, 419-420. Brown does not consider that Luke 2:6-7 reflects any circumstances of poverty which may have surrounded Jesus' birth. Luke alludes to a number of passages from the Old Testament to underscore the messianic character of the child who was born to Mary. Even if Brown is correct about Luke's allusions to Old Testament texts, this does not mean that the details of the story that Luke is telling do not paint a picture of Jesus, the Messiah, being born into poverty. This is part of the paradox of Jesus' messiahship.

father, Joseph was a *tekton,* a builder, a contractor, a skilled laborer. But Jesus left his family and occupation. He asked the same of those who wished to follow him. In Jesus' inaugural sermon, Luke has Jesus proclaim a year of jubilee (4:18) when the poor have their debts forgiven. During his ministry he had no place where he could lay his head (Matt 8:20; Lk 9:58). Throughout his life Jesus was able to dissociate himself from possessions because they accounted for nothing in terms of the kingdom he was called to proclaim. He challenges his followers to trust in God implicitly (Matt 6:25-34). His solidarity with the poor became complete during his passion when he died the death of a criminal. Paul calls this act of solidarity the taking on the form of a slave (Phil 2:7). It is among the least important members of the Christian community that Jesus is to be found today (Matt 25:31-36). Because of his own poverty, Jesus' call for detachment from every care and for complete trust in God (Matt 6:25-34; Lk 12:22-32) has an air of authenticity about it.

That Jesus himself was poor ought to be evident since his approach to poverty and wealth was not marked by asceticism or vague idealism. It exhibited the realism of the genuinely poor. Jesus allowed himself to be supported by generous women of means (Lk 8:1-3). He had no problem with the wealthy as long as they used their wealth for good such as the support of parents (Mk 7:9) or lending to those in need without expecting a profit (Matt 5:42). Evidently Jesus was fond of a good meal since he was criticized for being a glutton and a drunkard (Matt 11:19). Jesus criticized riches when they became the dominating force in a person's life, but he did not approach the issue of poverty and wealth like a fanatical ascetic or even like the people of Qumran. The gospels present Jesus as materially poor and his statements about the poor and the wealthy need to be heard from that perspective marked as it is by authenticity and realism.

Mark

Although the Gospel of Mark is not concerned about the poor as such, there are three instances of references to the poor in this gospel that merit attention. The first is the advice Jesus gives to a man who believed that living according to the Law was not enough (10:17-22). The man's question, "Good Teacher, what must I do to inherit eternal life?" would not have occurred to most observant Jews. They fully expected eternal life as a reward for the keeping of the Law. Jesus answers the query with the assertion that he understood the man's feelings of uneasiness. Jesus asserts that there is more to a person's relationship to God than what is circumscribed by the Law. The way to eternal life is to cast one's lot with him by becoming a disciple (v. 21). The way to discipleship is costly for it involves taking on the pattern of life set by Jesus, the poor man. The story ends with a statement explaining the man's failure to accept Jesus invitation as the result of his wealth (v. 23).

Verses 23-27 form an appendix to the story in which Jesus explains his words to the disciples because they find them difficult to understand and accept (vv. 24, 26).[5] This interchange between Jesus and his disciples fits very well into the larger context (9:30—10:31) in which Jesus is instructing the disciples concerning the cost of discipleship. After his second prediction of the passion (9:30-32), Jesus is trying to convince the disciples that they too will have to sacrifice and suffer just as he must. Jesus' commendation of the life of the poor then should not be seen as an idealization of the poor as such. It represents an opportunity to share the suffering of Jesus.

Next is Jesus' praise of the poor widow (12:41-44). The widow who puts in two copper coins into the Temple's treasury out of her need is the perfect foil to the scribes who exploit the poor (12:38-40). Although there were many good

[5]This same pattern is found in 4:1-9 (the Parable of the Sower) which is followed by an explanation of the parable to the disciples (vv. 13-20).

scribes, Jesus points to the crimes of a few. He contrasts the avarice of the evil scribes with the generosity of the widow who "out of her poverty, put in everything she had." There are parallels in Jewish sources to this incident.[6] These too praise the generosity of the poor.

The most difficult Marcan passage that deals with the poor comes in the incident of the anointing of Jesus in Bethany a few days before his crucifixion (14:1-9). Anointing with oil was a common enough practice of refreshment before a meal. Evidently such a practice was a bit too expensive for a number of people with whom Jesus was associated and the woman is criticized for her "extravagance." It was suggested that a better use of resources would have been to sell the oil and give the proceeds to the poor (v.5). Jesus deflects this criticism because he recognized the devotion of the woman.[7] He responds to the criticism of the supposed waste by stating: "For you always have the poor with you, and whenever you will, you can do good to them..." (v. 7a). Again this text reveals the realism of the poor, but it should not be read as if it were saying that poverty is something about which nothing can be done. The biblical tradition as a whole sees poverty as an evil exception to the divine plan. What is to be "normal" in this situation is the concern that moves people to be benevolent toward the poor. Mark does not attempt a thoroughgoing discussion of poverty here; the point of this story lies elsewhere. It ought not be used as an excuse to evade responsibility to the poor because it must be remembered that it was a poor man who spoke those words.

What is important to notice about all three instances in which the poor are mentioned in Mark's gospel is that Mark had the material poor in mind. There is no indication in this

---

[6]D. E. Nineham, *Saint Mark*. The Pelican Gospel Commentaries. (Baltimore: Penguin, 1963), p. 334.

[7]Mark sees another meaning in the anointing. He sees it as a token of Jesus' messiahship. That is why he places it here. John places it a few days earlier (John 12:1) and Luke provides a variant at a completely different point in Jesus' career (Luke 7:36-50).

gospel of any type of spiritualization of poverty or an idealization of the poor. The poor are objects of charity. Though wealth may be a danger and individual poor persons may be praised for their piety, none of these texts provide the poor with a special aura of holiness.

MATTHEW

Matthew uses two of the Marcan passages about the poor found within his own gospel. Matthew 19:16-21 reprises the story of the rich young man and 26:6-11, that of Jesus' anointing in Bethany. In neither case does Matthew appreciably change the sense of these stories as they relate to the poor. Two texts not found in Mark are the beatitude in Matthew 5:3 and the answer to the Baptist's question in 11:5.

Much has been said about the difference between Matthew's formula "Blessed are the poor in spirit" (5:3) as compared with Luke's "Blessed are you poor" (Lk 6:20). Supposedly Matthew's formula represents a kind of "spiritualization" of poverty. To understand what Matthew means it is necessary to study Matthew 5:3 in its own context. First of all, it is important to recognize that the people who are the subject of the beatitudes are people in physical distress (Matt 5:4, 6, 10). The message of the beatitudes is that the fortunes of these people will be reversed in God's time so that what appear as patterns of behavior that bring suffering and unhappiness in the present are revealed as those which bring status and salvation in God's kingdom in the future. The beatitudes exhibit the kind of belief in the reversal of fortunes that is characteristic of apocalyptic thought. Jesus believed that at present evil has perverted the designs that God had for the world but that the kingdom of God will bring a future which will witness the rectification of all that has been perverted. Because Jesus himself was poor, the situation of the economically oppressed would immediately suggest itself to Jesus as a symptom of the power of evil in this world. Jesus does not idealize poverty as such but uses it as a metaphor to describe a much more comprehensive reality.

There is a temptation to see the phrase "poor in spirit" as a kind of spiritualization of poverty. There is no real consensus on what "in spirit" means.[8] Perhaps Matthew 5:3 ought to be read in tandem with 5:5 "Blessed are the meek, for they shall inherit the earth." No doubt the Semitic word that lies behind the word "meek" is *'anawim.* Matthew 5:5 says that being among the *'anawim* (the poor)—now means that in the future one will inherit the earth, i.e. one's poverty will end. Matthew 5:3 also speaks about a reversal for the poor but one that is more eschatologically oriented. Those who are poor now will be part of the kingdom of heaven in the future. Matthew then does not so much "spiritualize" poverty as much as he sees the reversal of fortunes that comes with the kingdom includes more than the readjustment of socio-economic status in this world. In the future those who are poor now will gain the greatest possession of all.

The second distinctive use of the term "poor" in Matthew comes in 11:5. Through emissaries the imprisoned Baptist inquired whether Jesus might be "the one who is to come" (11:3). Instead of answering John's inquiry directly, Jesus invites the Baptist's messengers to consider what they have seen and heard (11:4). The rest of Jesus' reply (v. 5) is a montage made up of allusions to Isaiah 29:18-19; 35:5-6 and 61:1-2. Coming at the end of the list, "the poor have the good news preached to them" bears a certain emphasis as a sign that Jesus is indeed "the one who is to come." Since the biblical tradition sees God as the protector of the poor, the one who brings deliverance to the poor, the one who hears the cries of the poor, Jesus' mission to the poor is a clear sign that God is the power behind the words and deeds of Jesus.

Although Matthew is sometimes accused of "spiritualizing" the poor, that estimate of his work is inaccurate. What Matthew emphasizes is the eschatological dimension of Jesus' message. Preaching to the poor is the definitive sign of Jesus' unique role in the establishment of God's kingdom.

---

[8]Leander E. Keck, "Poor," *Interpreter's Dictionary of the Bible.* Supplementary volume, p. 674.

When that kingdom comes it will involve a reversal of fortunes for those impoverished and distressed now. As was the case with Mark, Matthew is thinking of the economically poor when he refers to "the poor" in his gospel. There is no basis for asserting that Matthew has spiritualized poverty or that he is talking about anyone other than the materially poor when he uses the term "poor" in his account of Jesus' life and ministry.

LUKE

While Mark and Matthew were not directly concerned about poverty, the theme of the rich and the poor is a significant one for Luke.[9] This evangelist has nine separate pericopes in which the poor are mentioned, and of these five are unique to Luke.

An obvious place to begin is with the Magnificat (1:46-55). In the prologue to his gospel (chapters 1-2) Luke presents all of the themes that he will develop in the rest of this two-volume work (Lk-Acts).[10] The Magnificat is found in the third scene (1:39-45) of that prologue which recounts the meeting between Mary and Elizabeth. This hymn sets out to explain the mutual greetings of the two women. Allusion to three social evils experienced by the people of Judah in the first century have been detected in this hymn: 1) foreign domination, 2) the diaspora of the Jews and 3) the oppression of the poor by the wealthy.[11] Allusions to ancient Israelite and early Jewish texts abound in the Magnificat so

[9]Robert Karris, O.F.M., "Poor and Rich: the Lukan *Sitz-im-Leben*," in *Perspectives on Luke-Acts*, C.H. Talbert, ed. (Association of Baptist Professors of Religion, 1978), pp. 112-125.

[10]Paul S. Minear, "Luke's Use of the Birth Stories," in *Studies in Luke-Acts*, L.E. Keck and J.L. Martyn, eds. (Nashville: Abingdon, 1966), p. 115.

[11]W.D. Davies, *Invitation to the New Testament*. (Garden City: Doubleday, 1966), p. 156.

its approach to dealing with these evils is somewhat eclectic.[12] It is clear, however, that the Magnificat deals with the evil of oppression by the wealthy by calling upon a common biblical motif: God's salvation of the lowly and the associated rejection of the mighty.[13]

In v. 48 ("for God has regarded the low estate of his handmaiden") Luke states explicitly an important theme of his gospel: the poor, the hungry, the oppressed have received God's favor while the rich and powerful have fallen. The most dramatic illustration of this truth is that a peasant maiden has been chosen to bear the Messiah. It is important to note that Mary's "low estate" is not simply a pious expression of humility. It reflects the social differentiation in first century society which placed Mary not among the powerful but among those without social position and prestige. According to the biblical tradition it is just such as these who can expect God to deliver them. In v. 52 the mighty are removed from their positions of power and the poor replace them. Not only are the powerful replaced but they are sent away empty, while the hungry poor are satisfied (v. 53). The social situation of his time and the biblical traditions that he reinterpreted allowed Luke to describe his conception of how God acts. Certainly Luke has the economically poor in mind but, of course, he casts his net beyond them to include all those in need of salvation. The poor are images of the wider circle of humanity that stands in need of salvation. That salvation is forthcoming because God responds to those in need.

The next place to go is Luke's beatitude: "Blessed are you poor, for yours is the kingdom of God" (6:20). In comparison with Matthew's version of this beatitude, it is much easier to claim that Luke was not speaking about some sort of "spiritual poverty," but rather material, economic poverty.

[12]There are allusions to Genesis 25:22-24; 2 Samuel 6:16; 2 Samuel 2:1-10; Isaiah 35:6; 40:9-10, 29-31; 41:8-10, 17-20; 42:1-4, 7; 49:1-7; 50:4-9; 52:13; 53:12; 61:1-3; Judges 5:24; Judith 13:18; Malachi 3:13; Zechariah 3:17; Psalm 111:9.

[13]See Genesis 24:35; 26:13; 41:52; Psalms 17, 49; Isaiah 4:2-3; Sirach 10:14; 11:1-13.

As was the case in earlier biblical traditions, the poor served as a particularly apt metaphor for those who had no hope except in God. They could expect nothing from this world so that they could perceive the claim of God more clearly. This does not necessarily mean that the poor actually recognized the nature of Jesus' mission any more than did the wealthy. Luke is simply using a familiar biblical metaphor to speak about the kind of attitude that helped lead people to accept Jesus. According to ancient Near Eastern tradition which the Bible accepts, the poor are under special divine protection, which is to be guaranteed on earth by the king. Jesus asserts that he is establishing God's kingdom in which the poor will enjoy the divine protection which is their right.

The reason the poor are blessed is because the kingdom of God will put an end to their poverty. Here Luke is not at all distant from Matthew; both exhibit an appreciation for an apocalyptic eschatology. Secondly, the poor are blessed because their very economic distress places them in a situation that makes responsiveness to the message of Jesus much less of a problem. This is made clear by the word Jesus utters against the rich (6:24-26). People of means are at risk in the kingdom because of their possessions.

Jesus' inaugural sermon at Nazareth quotes Isaiah 61:1-2 and underscores God's interest in people's physical, social and economic state (4:18). The poor of these texts are the materially poor to whom Jesus comes with a word of hope. Luke 7:22 states that this word has been carried out. In the first century the blind, the lame, the lepers, and the deaf certainly would belong to the category of the poor since they would have been unable to support themselves. Their physical problems made them poor. Jesus points out that his mission can be authenticated precisely by attending to the benefits these people have enjoyed through it. Again, the poor here must be the materially poor whether their poverty is caused by economic or physical factors.

In the Parable of the Great Supper (14:16-24) Luke discloses his concern for the poor. In Matthew's version (22:2-10), the servants are told to invite as many as they find (v. 9) to the wedding feast after the invited guests decline their invitations. In Luke, the servant is ordered to bring in "the poor, and maimed and blind and lame" (14:21). The original guests declined the invitation because they were too involved with their possessions (vv. 18-20). For Luke, this parable was part of Jesus' criticism of the religious elite who were not responsive to his mission. Rather than disqualifying Jesus as the one sent from God their lack of response confirmed the authenticity of Jesus' mission. According to Isaiah 55:1-3, the Messianic banquet was described as a meal of the poor. It is just these poor who are receptive to Jesus. The poor then once again are metaphors for those who will be saved. The kind of people who will enter the kingdom are those who see themselves as dependent upon the generosity of God just as the materially poor are dependent upon the generosity of other people. The metaphor would not be compelling unless it spoke about the materially poor.

One significant parable unique to Luke is the story of the Rich Man and Lazarus (16:19-31). In the parable there is no indication of any special guilt on the rich man's part except that he did not care for Lazarus. Similarly there is no special merit on Lazarus' part. He is a man incapacitated by physical ailments that reduced him to the status of a beggar. His very name, however, reminds the reader of the biblical tradition about God as protector of the poor.[14] The parable implies that the kingdom belongs to the poor while the rich may share in it if they treat the poor with kindness and benevolence. Although the parable is about the after-life, its purpose is to describe how the rich ought to lead their lives in the present.[15]

This parable is placed in a context of conflict with the Pharisees (see Lk 16:14-15). Once again the poor become paradigmatic figures for those who accept the message of salvation. The rich man represents the Pharisees who had

---

[14]Lazarus is a Hellenized form of the Hebrew name Eliezer which means "God helps."

[15]Similar parables are found in Egyptian and rabbinic tradition. See Joachim Jeremias, *The Parables of Jesus.* (N.Y.: Charles Scribner's Sons, 1963), p. 183.

their chance but refused to accept Jesus. It is important to note that this parable does not portray Lazarus as "spiritually poor," but confines its description to his physical and material status.

The story of Zaccheus (19:1-10) illustrates the truth of the foregoing parable. The rich man Zaccheus (v. 2) asserts that he will give half of his wealth to the poor (v. 8). This is tangible evidence of his repentance. Zaccheus is the only rich man who is saved in Luke. Apparently Luke believed that people of means can be saved only by a kind of repentance that is demonstrated by giving to the poor.[16] Zaccheus' act of repentance would have meaning only if Luke refers to the economically poor.

Zaccheus was willing to forego his wealth for the sake of the kingdom. Luke, however, knew of another man who was not so willing. The tradition behind 18:18-30 (the rich ruler) is common to the synoptics (see Matt 19:16-30 and Mk 10:17-31). Luke was not unique in pointing out the dangers to salvation that wealth brought with itself. He, however, accentuated the warning regarding the proper use of wealth. But did Luke call for a total renunciation of possessions on the part of those who wished to be disciples of Jesus? Luke is probably quite close to Jesus' own teaching here because total renunciation is most compatible with the eschatological orientation of Jesus' message, yet renunciation is only half of the story. The rich man was called to place all his trust in God by selling his possessions. He was also asked to use the profits from the sale to benefit the poor. Jesus was not merely looking for a proper attitude towards possession; he deemed proper action equally important.[17] In explaining the failure of the man to pick up on the challenge offered by Jesus, Matthew and Mark note that the young man "had many possessions." Luke, however, states that he was "very

---

[16]In Luke 12:32-33 the disciple is told to give alms with the expectation that this will bring the one who gives alms treasure in heaven.

[17]Luke also has John the Baptist calling for concrete acts of benevolence toward the poor as signs of repentance. See 3:10-14.

rich" (v. 23). Luke keeps the social distinction between rich and poor quite clear. A striking contrast to the rich man is the poor widow whose gift of two copper coins to the Temple's treasury was "all the living she had" (21:1-4). Luke then uses the contrast between the wealthy and the poor as an indicator of people's attitudes towards Jesus and the message he brings from God.[18]

The command to give to the poor (18:22) does not present any indication of an idealization of the poor. The command to give one's wealth to the poor would contradict an attitude that regarded poverty as somehow virtuous in itself. With such a view of poverty, the poor could only be corrupted by such acts of largess. The primary focus in Luke is not the need to recognize that discipleship takes precedence over wealth. That the rich man was unwilling to surrender his wealth for the sake of the kingdom provides ample testimony to the danger of wealth, while it implicitly shows the value of poverty since the poor person would never have to face the kind of decision faced by the rich one. In a sense it was much easier for the poor woman to give her two copper coins than it was for the rich man to divest himself of his possessions.

The absence of references to the poor in the Acts of the Apostles is strange if "the poor" were an important theme for Luke. But Luke's conception of salvation history makes this absence understandable. The Magnificat's assertion that the rich will be sent away and those of low degree exalted has taken place according to Luke. The reversal of fortunes has taken place in Jesus, so that Luke's use of the poor as symbols of those who wait for salvation is no longer necessary. Salvation has indeed come. Luke, of course, does not forget the materially poor since he mentions almsgiving a number of times, and widows, one of the traditional categories of the poor, receive special treatment in Acts 6:1-6. In Acts 4:34 Luke notes that the problem of indigence did not exist in the Jerusalem church because members of that

---

[18]Joseph A. Fitzmyer, S.J., *The Gospel according to Luke I-IX.* The Anchor Bible, 28. (Garden City: Doubleday, 1981), p. 250.

community shared their food and possessions though Acts 24:16-17 may refer to the collection which Paul took up for the poor of the Jerusalem Christian community (see 1 Cor 16:1-4; 2 Cor 8:23).

There are two crucial texts from Acts that help broaden an understanding of Luke's views of poverty. The first is Acts 2:44-45:

> "And all who believed were together and had all things in common; and they sold their possessions and goods and distributed them to all, as any had need."

A second text is Acts 4:32, 34-35:

> "Now the company of those who believed were of one heart and soul, and no one said that any of the things which he possessed was his own, but they had everything in common.... There was not a needy person among them, for as many as were possessors of lands or houses sold them, and brought the proceeds of what was sold and laid it at the apostles' feet; and distribution was made to each as any had need."

Luke here presents a picture of the first Christian community that Hellenists would find attractive. Pythagoras, Plato and Aristotle are among the Greek philosophers who spoke highly of friends who shared their goods with one another.[19] Yet it is clear that the picture that Luke paints of the first Christian community is not made up of colors taken exclusively from Hellenism. Acts 4:34 ("There was not a needy person among them...") reproduces the Septuagint rendering of Deuteronomy 15:4.[20] The thrust of this text is that in the final days all Israel will observe the Law and consequently poverty will no longer exist. The early Church

---

[19]Jacques Dupont, O.S.B., "Community of Goods in the Early Church," in his *The Salvation of the Gentiles.* (N.Y.: Paulist, 1979), pp. 87-91.

[20]*Ibid.,* p. 92.

considered itself to be the true Israel living in the final times and therefore it does not hesitate to apply this text to itself. That no one in that community was suffering in poverty should have been a sign that Moses' promise had been fulfilled.

The practice of sharing a community of goods is certainly quite opposed to a kind of selfish individualism that makes the possession of private goods as the absolute basis of economic life. Luke reveals a community of people who put their goods at the disposal of those in need without reservation.

Luke's use of the word "poor" focuses on the economically poor; however, Luke does not idealize the poor simply because they are poor. The evangelist notes that they are heirs of the Kingdom—but not the only ones. The rich can inherit the Kingdom as well if they become disciples. Unfortunately wealth and the self-sufficiency it provides often hinder people of means from becoming disciples. Once they become believers they give expression to their new life by sharing their goods with those in need. That is why Luke addresses the rich more than he does the poor. He warns them, admonishes them and challenges them because they face temptations that the poor do not know because of their poverty. Joseph A. Fitzmyer believes that Luke's advice regarding wealth is somewhat ambivalent.[21] On the one hand, the evangelist is moderate when he advocates a prudent use of possessions (3:11; 12:42; 16:8). On the other hand, Luke also betrays a more radical attitude toward material goods (6:35; 9:3; 10:4; 12:33; 14:33; 16:13). In spite of this ambivalence, Luke makes it clear that economic poverty, which is the product of injustice, is not something which the disciple can countenance. Finally Luke portrays Jesus as someone who is poor and concerned about the poor, as is evident from the first words Jesus says in the course of his ministry (4:16-30).[22]

---

[21]Fitzmyer, *The Gospel according to Luke I-IX,* pp. 249-250.
[22]Keck, "Poor," p. 674.

JOHN

The poor are mentioned only twice in John's gospel—both times in connection with Judas' supposed concern for them. The first of these occurs in 12:1-8 which is John's story about the anointing at Bethany. In the accounts of Matthew and Mark, unnamed witnesses to the anointing criticize the extravagance of the woman who anoints Jesus' feet with expensive perfume. In John's version of the story it is Judas alone who complains (v. 5). He observes that the perfume could have been sold and the proceeds given to the poor. The evangelist observes in an aside that Judas was not really concerned about the poor; rather, he was a thief (v. 6). John implies that if the perfume had been sold, the proceeds would have been misappropriated by Judas. The story does not intend to deal with the poor. Its focus is on Judas, one of Jesus' closest associates. Obviously his betrayal of Jesus required some explanation, which John provides by pointing out Judas' avarice. The justification for Mary's action given by Jesus in v. 8 is identical with Matthew 26:11.[23] This verse indicates that Mary's act of kindness is given to Jesus in view of his impending death and burial. It is an extraordinary act of kindness, while almsgiving is a normal expectation of every Jew. That is the significance of Jesus' remark, "the poor you will always have with you" (v. 8). It is not meant to describe poverty as a normal feature of society.

The one other time the poor are mentioned is in 13:29 which appears as another one of John's asides given in the course of recounting Jesus' prediction of his betrayal by Judas. When Jesus sent Judas out of the cenacle, the disciples merely thought that as the keeper of the common purse Judas was being sent to give something to the poor, as was customary on the night of Passover.[24]

[23]This verse is not found in some ancient texts of John's Gospel. This together with the fact that Matthew's version is reproduced rather than Mark's may indicate a later scribal addition from the more traditional Matthew.

[24]Joachim Jeremias, *The Eucharistic Words of Jesus.* rev. ed. (N.Y.: Scribner, 1966), p. 54.

While neither of these texts deals with the poor directly, both look upon almsgiving as a normal activity expected of every person. The almost total absence of "the poor" from the Fourth Gospel indicates that its author did not have any special view of the poor nor did he exhibit any awareness of a unique "spirituality" of the poor.

PAUL

The Apostle does not seem to be aware of any "spirituality" of the poor. Such a motif is simply not developed in his letters. Perhaps this is because the Jews of the Diaspora and their proselytes who were the objects of Paul's preaching generally did not come from the poor of society.[25] When Paul alludes to social tensions within the communities he founded, he does not directly mention "the poor" (see Rom 12:6-8; 2 Cor 8:14; Gal 6:10). When Paul speaks about equality in Christ and the destruction of all social barriers (Gal 3:27-28; Col 3:11), he does not mention the rich and poor.

But Paul does not ignore the poor. In his account of how the Jerusalem community recognized Paul's authority (Gal 2:1-10), he mentions a duty which that Church imposed upon him. The Apostle was told to "remember the poor" (v. 10). Paul also adds that he accepted this obligation eagerly. A number of times Paul mentions a collection he took up as a way to fulfill that obligation (1 Cor 16:1; 2 Cor 8:4; 9:1-2; Rom 12:13) and in Romans 15:25 he states that the poor of

[25]Philip Seidensticker, O.F.M., "St. Paul and Poverty," in *The Gospel and Poverty,* p. 99. In the view of the author if the Pauline communities were to be ranked according to modern standards, they would fall into the category of well-off middle class (p. 100). See also Martin Hengel, *Property and Riches in the Early Church.* (Philadelphia: Fortress, 1974), p. 37.

More recent studies modify that conclusion somewhat and suggest that Paul's communities were made up of people from across the social spectrum with the exception of the very lowest and highest strata. See Wayne Meeks, *The First Urban Christians.* (New Haven: Yale, 1983) and Gerd Theissen, *The Social Setting of Pauline Christianity.* (Philadelphia: Fortress, 1982).

the Jerusalem Church were to benefit from this collection.[26] Paul commends the churches of Macedonia which contributed to this collection despite their own poverty (2 Cor 8:2). He tries to motivate the Corinthians to do their part when he states that Christ became poor so that by his poverty the Corinthians might become rich (2 Cor 8:9). The generosity of believers toward the poor is to testify to the grace that they have received through Jesus. The Apostle then describes generosity towards the poor as imitation of Christ.

The Apostle refers to himself as "poor": "...but as servants of God we commend ourselves...as poor, yet making many rich; as having nothing, and yet possessing everything" (2 Cor 6:4, 10). These words are just one part of a highly rhetorical and emotional defense of his ministry by Paul. The terms "poor" and "having nothing" are quite enigmatic. What Paul wants to emphasize is not so much his personal circumstances as the effects of his ministry on the lives of the Corinthians.

Paul's attitude toward the poor was probably colored by his expectations regarding the Parousia, the imminent return of Christ. The Apostle's eschatological orientation does not allow him to deal at any great length with socio-economic problems. If people work, the lack of a comfortable life will at least be tolerable. Paul sets himself up as a model:

> "For you yourselves know how you ought to imitate us; we were not idle when we were with you, we did not eat any one's bread without paying, but with toil and labor we worked night and day, that we might not burden any

---

[26]Seidensticker, *"Saint Paul and Poverty"*, pp. 88-92 insists that when Paul uses the term "poor" in Romans 15:26, he is not speaking of the economically poor but he simply uses a self-designation of the Jerusalem Church. If the collection was not to relieve the needs of the poor, what was its purpose?

See Keck, "The Poor among the Saints in Jewish Christianity," which denies that "The Poor" was ever a self-designation used by the early Church.

of you. It was not because we have not that right, but to give you in our conduct an example to imitate." (2 Thess 3:7-9)

Here Paul reflects his Greco-Roman background that considered dependence upon the charity of others as repugnant.[27] He was unwilling to live off of alms even though he had a right to do so because of his position as a minister of the gospel. In Philippians 4:10, Paul implies that his independence is important to him. He does not wish to be dependent upon the Philippian church. To do so he has learned how to be content with little. Paul is willing to make the necessary renunciations not because he values poverty in and of itself but because he values his independence more than a comfortable existence.

There is one place where Paul sounds like a revolutionary. This is when he was speaking to the Church at Corinth. Evidently there were social differences among the members of that community. The Hellenistic world was quite class conscious and the divisions within Corinthian society spilled over into the community of faith: "... when you assemble as a church, I hear that there are divisions among you..." (1 Cor 11:18). Wealthy members of that community kept to themselves, feasted on their own food at the Lord's Supper and neglected the hungry. Paul condemns such behavior because it disrupted the unity of the body of Christ (1 Cor 11:22, 29). The wealthy Corinthians were introducing their unjust social system into the Church. This Paul had rejected by describing how God acts towards the poor: "God chose what is low and despised in the world, even things that are not, to bring to nothing things that are..." (1 Cor 1:28). Paul states that the community of faith represents God's intervention to overturn the existing unjust social order. The social tensions of Corinthian society must not be allowed to spill over into the church.

---

[27]See Hengel's discussion of "self-sufficiency" in Greco-Roman philosophy in his *Property and Riches in the Early Church, op. cit.,* pp. 54-59.

There is no evidence to suggest that Paul saw any theological value to material poverty. In addition the Apostle did not idealize the poor. While Paul is willing to provide alms for the Church in Jerusalem, he is unwilling to allow collections to be taken up for himself even though he has a right to support from the Churches. Paul does not wish to live off alms. He prefers to work and will be content with little in order to preserve his independence. Paul does, however, encourage people to be generous to those in need (2 Cor 9:6-9) and apparently he regarded giving to the poor an important virtue (1 Cor 13:3).

OTHER NEW TESTAMENT TEXTS

None of the other texts from the New Testament appear to develop any type of "spirituality" of the poor. Whenever these texts speak about the poor, it is usually in terms of their being objects of charity (Eph 4:28; 1 Tim 6:17-19; James 1:27; 2:14-17; 1 Jn 3:17). The poor in these texts are the economically poor. They are not images of the believer; they are those who depend upon the charity of others to survive.

James 2:1-7 is more of a rebuke to the rich than it is a glorification of the poor. It reflects a situation in which the poor were not being held in very high esteem because of the entry of wealthy people into the community. This James regarded as detestable. To bolster his argument he observes that "God has chosen the poor in the world to be rich in faith" (2:5). James insisted that the social differentiation between poor and rich within the community must stop. In 5:1-6 James launches another scathing attack on the rich. This time he describes their role in general society. He accuses them of unjust activity with an intensity that rivals even Amos.

The Book of Revelation mentions the poor twice. In 3:17, the usage is metaphorical. The wealth of Laodicea is revealed as poverty. The city was known for its banking activities and industry but because of the indifference of the Christian community, the city is really "poor." In 13:16, the book speaks about all humanity as being marked by the beast. The rich and the poor are among the categories of people who will be marked. Here rich and poor are used quite literally.

Conclusion

When the New Testament speaks of "the poor," it refers to the materially poor. The actions of some of the poor are praised but poverty as such is not idealized as a state which gives one special access to God. The most that can be said about poverty is that it eliminates one type of temptation to dismiss Jesus' call to repentance—the temptation that comes through the self-sufficiency that wealth provides. One way for people of means to give a tangible sign of their repentance is for them to distribute their wealth to people in need. Despite its eschatological orientation, nothing in the New Testament leads to the conclusion that material poverty is something that can be ignored or that its existence ought to be accepted fatalistically. Indeed the Gospels present Jesus as one of the poor and any observations Jesus makes about poverty and the poor need to be understood as statements of a poor person. Responding to Jesus' call for conversion enables the disciple to hear the call of the biblical tradition for justice. It impels the disciples to sell what they have in order to give to the poor. Paul gives no evidence of any transvaluation of poverty into some sort of a spiritual reality. He advises people to work to support themselves and to be happy with a less than comfortable existence. The Apostle also asks people to support the poor of the Church in Jerusalem.

The New Testament does not speak with the passion of the Hebrew prophets regarding social injustice except in a few places such as James 2:1-6 and 5:1-6. It does however speak quite a lot about a kind of solidarity within the community of faith that makes social injustice unthinkable. Above all, it presents the life and teaching of one who was able to live without the security of possessions and power. It challenges his followers to do the same.

Select Bibliography

Boerma, Conrad, *The Rich, the Poor and the Bible.* Philadelphia: Westminster, 1980.

Guinan, Michael D., ed. *Gospel Poverty: Essays in Biblical Theology.* Chicago: Franciscan Herald Press, 1977.

_____, *Gospel Poverty: Witness to the Risen Christ.* N.Y.: Paulist, 1981.

Hengel, Martin, *Property and Riches in the Early Church.* Philadelphia: Fortress, 1974.

Kee, Howard C., *Christian Origins in Sociological Perspective.* Philadelphia: Fortress, 1980.

Malina, Bruce J., *The New Testament World: Insights from Cultural Anthropology.* Atlanta: Knox, 1981.

Meeks, Wayne, *The First Urban Christians: The Social World of the Apostle Paul.* New Haven: Yale, 1983.

Theissen, Gerd, *The Sociology of Early Palestinian Christianity.* Philadelphia: Fortress, 1982.

9

The Poor in the Rabbinic Tradition

Introduction

The attitude of the rabbis toward poverty is somewhat ambivalent. Because poverty was so widespread both in Palestine and in the Diaspora, it was seen as a permanent part of Jewish experience and so there were attempts to give it a positive value. One rabbi in commenting on Deuteronomy 15:11 ("For the poor will never cease out of the land") intimated that poverty will be a feature of the messianic age:

> "The only difference between this world and the days of the Messiah is that slavery to governments will cease." (bBerakot 34b) [1]

[1] In the citations of texts from the Talmud and Mishnah, the prefixed "b" indicates that the text is taken from the Babylonian Talmud. An English translation is available: *The Babylonian Talmud*. I. Epstein, ed. 35 vols. (London: Soncino Press, 1935-1952). A prefixed "M." indicates that the text is taken from this Mishnah. An English translation is available; *The Mishnah*. Translated by Herbert Danby. (Oxford: The University Press, 1967). The words following these prefixes are the names of the particular tractates being cited.

This rabbi believed that even in the messianic age there will be poverty and the opportunity for charity. On the other hand, poverty was also seen as a great evil and a curse from God. Jewish piety took its cue from the Torah and the prophets and did its best to alleviate the burdens of the poor. Despite these efforts there still remained economic disparity among the Jews which gave rise to social problems.

Poverty according to the Rabbis

In antiquity Palestine possessed enough natural wealth to support its population well but most people in the first few hundred years of the common era lived in poverty.[2] A second century Rabbi lamented: "The daughters of Israel are comely but poverty destroys their comeliness!" (M. Nedarim 9:10). Certainly one cause of this poverty was the almost continuous wars that were fought in Palestine from the Maccabean Revolution (167 B.C.) to the Second Revolt against Rome (A.D. 135). These wars together with the heavy burden of taxation made it difficult for the ordinary Jew to do well economically in Palestine. It was for this reason that poverty was not seen as an ideal but rather a punishment from God. The situation in the Diaspora was not very much different. Again political unrest and taxation made life difficult. The Talmud describes the economic situation of the Jews in the eastern Diaspora; "Of ten measures of poverty which descended to the world, Babylonia took nine" (bKiddushim, 49b). It further notes that the Jews celebrated their feasts with extraordinary joy because they provided a little relief from the burdens of poverty (bShabbat, 145b).

In some circles, poverty was looked upon as the worst possible disaster:

> "There is nothing harder in the world than poverty; for it is the hardest of all the sufferings in the world. Con-

[2]Salo W. Baron, *A Social and Religious History of the Jews.* 2nd ed. (N.Y.: Columbia University Press, 1952), p. 164.

> sequently Job prayed: 'Lord, I will accept all the suffering in the world but not poverty.'" (Exodus Rabbah 31:12)[3]

One rabbi classified the poor along with the lepers and the blind (see bNedarim 64b). To support their contention that poverty was a curse the rabbis often cited Proverbs 15:15: "All the days of the poor (*'ani*) are evil, but a cheerful heart has a continual feast."

There are a number of positive statements about poverty in rabbinic tradition. One text in the Talmud read::

> "...the Holy One, Blessed be He went through all the virtues in order to bestow them upon Israel and found none more becoming than poverty...." (bHagigah, 9b)

Another Talmudic text admonishes people to care for the poor since from them comes Torah (bNedarim, 81a). Although the notion was not mentioned widely among the rabbis there was still an awareness that the poor are the primary objects of God's concern (Exodus Rabbah 31:13). Some Jewish ascetics and mystics did glorify poverty but their approach to this issue did not achieve wide acceptance outside their own followers. In general, the rabbis did not idealize poverty.[4]

Though the tradition often portrays some of the early rabbis as poor and as supporting themselves by manual and even unskilled labor, the same tradition asserts that they finally achieved not only a great reputation for their learning but also economic prosperity. Their prosperity was partially enabled by their exemption from Roman taxes—a privilege granted by the Emperor Antoninus Pius and continued even by Christian emperors. Sometimes the members of the community resented the extra burden this privilege meant for themselves. In the third century the people of Sepphoris

---

[3]This work is available in *The Midrash Rabbah*. 3rd ed. H. Freedman and Maurice Simon eds. (London: Soncino, 1961). 10 vols.

[4]Brammel, *TDNT*, v. 6, p. 902.

(a city near Nazareth) opposed the rabbinic ordination of Rabbi Hanina because he was a wealthy landowner and his property would be taken off the tax rolls.[5]

Responsibility for the Poor

Despite an ambivalent attitude toward poverty as such, Jewish tradition is uniform in its social concern for the poor. In the rabbinic period there developed an emphasis on voluntary charity towards the poor rather than the protection of their rights according to legislation in the Torah.[6] According to a saying ascribed to the high priest Simon (200 B.C.), the world is sustained by three things: "by the Torah, by the [Temple] service, and by deeds of loving kindness" (M. Pirke Aboth 1:3). Jewish communities made this value concrete by developing a system of caring for the needs of the poor. One such system is described in chapter four of the Tosefta Peah.[7] Each town had two men who collected for the poor on Friday before the Sabbath began. A committee of three other men were responsible for investigating the needs of the poor. In cases when the collection did not meet those needs, the members of the committee made up the difference themselves or sought a loan. Out of these funds the poor received money for food for the coming week. Clothing was furnished when needed. Visitors from another village who were out of funds were given aid. The community supported the orphans of the village as well. What was unique about this system was that people of means who fell on bad times would receive the kind of food and clothing to which they had become accustomed. All this was to be carried on with consideration for the feelings of the poor:

[5]Baron, vol. 2, p. 241.

[6]See Brammel, *TDNT,* v. 6, p. 900.

[7]See George Foot Moore, *Judaism in the First Centuries of the Christian Era.* (N.Y.: Schocken, 1971), pp. 174-176.

For an English translation of the Tosefta see *The Tosefta,* translated by Jacob Neusner. (N.Y.: Ktav, 1977-81), 6 vols.

"God stands together with the poor man at the door and one should therefore consider whom one is confronting." (Leviticus Rabbah 34:9)

All people were required to support these collections according to the measure of their ability, but people were not to impoverish themselves in the process of helping those in need. To protect people limits were set. The least that was to be given to the poor was two percent of one's income; the most, twenty percent.[8]

Social Conflict within Jewish Community

In the biblical period and in the years before the common era, there was a great disparity between the rich and the poor. This is quite clear from the literature. The situation changed in the period after the first revolt against Rome (A.D. 70). All Jews suffered because of the devastation which came because of that war. A new division developed within the community between those who considered that they were instructed in the Law and careful in its observance and those who were considered to be the ignorant and negligent—the so-called *'am ha'aretz* (the people of the land). Because the observant considered "the people of the land" to be ritually unclean, they avoided all contact with them. Meals could not be taken in their homes, they could not serve as witnesses in a trial, marriage between the two classes was forbidden. Worst of all, "the people of the land" did not receive support during difficult times (cf. bSanhedrin, 92a). The result of this social differentiation within the Jewish community was that "the people of the land" hated the observant Jews more than their gentile oppressors (see bPesahim 49b). Tensions between these groups sometimes resulted in violence and certainly had a role in the rise of

---

[8]Hengel, *Property and Riches in the Early Church*, p. 20; Baron, vol. 2, p. 271.

certain Jewish sects. One of the latter was the Karaite movement which arose in the eighth century A.D. It rejected the authority of the rabbis and their oral law and accepted only the Scriptures as authoritative. Central to their thought was the glorification of the poor with whom they identified themselves as they reflected upon texts such as Isaiah 29:19; 32:7; Zephaniah 3:12; Zechariah 11:11.[9]

There were class distinctions within Diaspora Jewry as well, although they were not based on questions of Jewish observance. In the Diaspora the Jews were integrated within the local economic structures. When problems arose within particular areas of the Diaspora, Jews tended to side not with their fellow Jews but with the members of their particular economic class.[10] One exception to this pattern was the responsibility all Jews felt to ransom Jewish slaves.

Conclusion

It is striking that the only Jews who explicitly take up the ideology of the poor as found in some of the prophets form a marginal group (the Karaites). In rabbinic Judaism poverty undergoes no transvaluation. Poverty was considered to be an evil despite occasional positive statements about it. The poor are treated more as objects of charity than they are as those who stand in a special relationship with God. The rabbis do not idealize the poor; they do not value poverty. For the rabbis, poverty is always an economic reality. Even in the few positive statements about the poor, their poverty never takes on a "spiritual" reality. Probably this was because the Jewish community in Palestine and in the Diaspora was poor for the most part. Social conflict took place on another level—that of observance. In rabbinic tradition the poor are those who experience material need.

[9]See N. Wieder, "The Qumran Sectaries and the Karaites," *Jewish Quarterly Review* 47 (1956-57), pp. 283-289.

[10]Baron, vol. 1, p. 281.

The clear response to that need according to the rabbis is acts of charity.

Select Bibliography

Kadushin, Max, *The Rabbinic Mind.* N.Y.: Jewish Theological Seminary of America, 1952.

Moore, George Foot, *Judaism in the First Centuries of the Christian Era.* 3 vols. Cambridge: Harvard University Press, 1927-30.

Neusner, Jacob, *Invitation to the Talmud.* N.Y.: Harper & Row, 1973.

Schechter, Solomon, *Aspects of Rabbinic Theology.* N.Y.: Schocken Books, 1961.

Viviano, Benedict, O.P., *Study as Worship: Aboth and the New Testament.* Leiden: Brill, 1978.

Conclusion

Attempting a synthesis of what the biblical tradition says about the poor is risky and almost foolhardy. After all, this tradition developed over more than one thousand years. It reflects varying circumstances of time and place. It is the product of very different types of experience and exhibits an amazing variety of ways of reflecting on that experience. Yet there have emerged some common affirmations and negations about poverty in the biblical tradition. The diversity that is so obvious in the Hebrew Scriptures, the inter-testamental literature, the New Testament and the rabbis is not of such a kind that makes it impossible to draw some conclusions about what the biblical tradition says about poverty.

First of all, the tradition is unanimous in asserting that material, economic poverty is a scandal, that it should not exist, that it is not in accord with the divine will. While, the tradition is not unanimous in its explanations for the origin of poverty, that is not the most important point to be made about the scandal of poverty. What is essential is that believers recognize that poverty results from decisions that people make. Poverty just does not happen; it happens because people make it happen. While sometimes these decisions can be laid at the door of the poor themselves, the predominant assertion made by the tradition is that the avarice and greed of the wealthy lead them to unjustly deprive some people of what they need for an existence without dehumanizing need. There is no question that the biblical tradition recognizes the evil of economic oppression. In the face of this oppression, this tradition affirms that God is the protector of those who are unjustly deprived of their access to the bounty of the earth and the fruits of their labor. The challenge offered to believers is to imitate the character of God and enable the poor to overcome the oppression that they experience in their lives.

Secondly, the biblical tradition finds the experience of the poor an apt metaphor for the universal need for salvation. The poor come to depend upon God because they cannot depend upon themselves, since most often they are powerless to change their situation. They cannot depend upon the wealthy because it is the wealthy who create and maintain their poverty. The poor have only one choice and that is to depend upon God. When people begin to recognize their need for salvation, the language of the poor becomes so appropriate. After all the wealthy stand in need before God just as the poor do. When the biblical tradition uses the language of the poor to speak about the universal experience of human poverty before God, it never denies the evil of material poverty. It never overlooks the injustice that creates oppression. It never suggests that poverty and oppression be ignored in favor of some sort of "spiritual poverty." In addition the biblical tradition does not idealize the poor as having some sort of special access to God. All people are called to repentance, and anyone—rich or poor—can resist that call. Though the Bible uses the cries of the poor to speak about the universal human need of God, it does not confer an aura of holiness around the poor nor does it ever denigrate the need to overcoming the forces that create and sustain injustice and oppression.

There are some consequences to both conclusions. First, if the biblical tradition regards material, economic poverty as a perversion of the divine will, believers cannot countenance its continued existence. This would be nothing less than acquiescing to the continued degradation and exploitation of the oppressed. Secondly, if the biblical tradition uses the language of the poor to speak about the human condition before God, then this metaphor calls for an authentic expression in the lives of believers. "Spiritual poverty" becomes authentic by incarnating itself in material poverty. "Spiritual poverty" calls for a modification of the way believers own and use economic goods. It involves more than simply acts of benevolence towards the poor, but it requires a transformation of the believer's life-style.

Though the Bible consistently describes poverty as an evil, it can become an act of liberation and redemption if it leads to the end of human alienation and exploitation. Voluntary poverty can become redemptive if it leads to genuine solidarity with the economically poor and commitment to overcoming their oppression and misery. The idealization of poverty must not lead to accepting an oppressive situation, but rather it ought to lead believers to opposing poverty as the evil that the Bible reveals it to be. In other words, "spiritual poverty" must lead to solidarity with the economically poor in their protest against oppression. It expresses itself through prayer to the God who takes the side of the poor against their oppressors. This is the one way that believers can justify using the language of the poor in their own prayer. For Christian believers, this solidarity with the poor is a genuine imitation of Christ, for it involves taking on the effects of human sin in order to liberate people from that sin and its terrible effects.

In today's world standing with the poor is very often a political act. Certainly there is always room for those who wish to express their solidarity with the poor through individual acts of benevolence. The poor and oppressed certainly need people like Mother Teresa of Calcutta, whose identification with the poor is complete. The poor need those who staff shelters for the homeless, food pantries for the hungry, day-care centers for the working poor. On the other hand, the poor today are resisting the structures of society that institutionalize poverty. In some circumstances, this resistance is expressed through public advocacy, lobbying, protesting and other forms of political action. In other circumstances such as in Latin America, South Africa and Afghanistan, this resistance takes the form of revolution against the intractable forces of oppression. These circumstances require from believers a new form of voluntary poverty that goes beyond living a "simple life-style." How then can believers continue to use the language of the poor to express their self-understanding if they are unwilling to stand with the poor in their action against injustice? The biblical tradition will not allow believers to be satisfied with attitudes of benevolence towards the poor. What is needed to guarantee authenticity are *actions*. But the Church calls people to conversion—not to revolution. In other words, those who would use the language of the poor in their prayer need to have a change of heart so that they can stand alongside the poor. More than this they themselves can become poor. They will become thereby instruments of justice and liberation.

The Bible can help shape an authentic response to poverty today. First of all, it is clear than any disregard and devaluation of the material poverty and concomitant concentration on "spiritual" poverty is contrary to biblical tradition. Similarly radical pronouncements and scathing criticisms of injustice and oppression that are not backed up by action do not exhibit the kind of conversion that the Gospel calls for. Finally the biblical tradition does not allow believers to leave social justice to political entities. The community of faith ought to provide a model of a society that is founded on solidarity rather than on conflict between social classes. The biblical tradition assumes that the community of faith ought to take action on behalf of the poor. Without this action on behalf of the poor, the community loses its reason for existence as the people of Israel and Judah discovered. In fact, the very existence of the poor indicates that the community has not been living up to its responsibilities. It is even worse if it abandons the poor to their fate.

Too often texts like Deuteronomy 15:11 "...the poor will never cease out of the land" (see also Matt 26:11; Mk 14:7; Jn 12:8) have been read as expressions of fatalism—as if poverty were a part of the natural order of things. When these texts are read against the wider backdrop of the biblical tradition, it is not poverty but mutual concern that is to be a normal pattern of the community's life. The Torah makes significant efforts at insuring that justice is done for the poor. The prophets criticize the people of ancient Israel for ignoring their responsibilities to the poor and making poverty to be a permanent part of ancient Israelite life. The reason "the poor will never cease out of the land" is because of people's failure to end poverty. People have created poverty; they ought to be able to end it.

The last word is directed at the work of Albert Gelin, P.S.S. whose classic, *The Poor of Yahweh,* has set the tone for the discussion of poverty in the Bible since it first appeared. His work attempted to describe how "poverty of spirit" became the dominant pattern of ancient Israel's response to God. He described how the poor are God's clients, how poverty came to mean the ability to welcome God and humility before God. He wished to show how the biblical tradition makes a transition from seeing poverty as a social problem to a religious metaphor. Above all he wished to demonstrate that this transition moved the center of attention away from material poverty to poverty of spirit.[1] Much of what Father Gelin wrote remains quite as valid and insightful today as when it was first written. The one concern of this book has been to show that the biblical tradition never minimizes or ignores material poverty and the real poor in society. Whenever the Bible uses the language of the poor, it is calling for justice and for an end to oppression. The very metaphor "the poor of Yahweh" can have its intended effect only if people know what it means to be materially poor. The community of faith can ignore material, economic poverty only at the risk of missing its call to stand

[1]See Gelin, *The Poor of Yahweh,* p. 26.

at the side of those whose cries God hears. The community of faith needs to make itself poor in order to use the language of the poor authentically. The resources of the community will be marshalled in order to bring an end to poverty. Gelin himself said as much when he wrote: "Without pretending to extract from the Bible an economic treatise, we have no right to forget the social results of its religious principles."[2] The way to insure this is for the community of faith to stand with the poor as God does.

[2]*Ibid.*, p. 113.

Subject Index

Author Index

Biblical Index

Intertestamental Literature

Qumran Texts

New Testament

Rabbinic Literature